The LANGUAGE *of* GLOBAL MARKETING

wmpease@RapportTranslations.com

ISBN: 978-1-7365614-0-9 (print)
ISBN: 978-1-7365614-1-6 (ebook)

Ordering Information:
Special discounts are available on quantity purchases by corporations, associations, and others. For details, contact www.wendypease.com or wmpease@RapportTranslations.com, +1-978-443-2540

David and Robert
I love you, my happy crabs...

and

Linda and Lisa
My Guiding Lights

The LANGUAGE *of* GLOBAL MARKETING

TRANSLATE YOUR
DOMESTIC STRATEGIES INTO
INTERNATIONAL SALES AND PROFITS

Wendy MacKenzie Pease

CONTENTS

INTRODUCTION

When I was in third and fourth grade, my family lived in Shanhua, Taiwan, in a small farming village about an hour and a half away from the nearest small city of Tainan. My father specialized in agriculture research and held a position at the newly opened Asian Vegetable Research and Development Center. We did not speak Mandarin or know how to write in Chinese characters; body language was the only way we could communicate with those around us.

Those years were among my first experiences with language and the challenges that can come with it—something that I built my career around. Our mission at Rapport International (www.rapporttranslations.com) is to connect people across languages and cultures for a peaceful and prosperous world, so it seemed natural for me to write a book to share my knowledge on transitioning from outbound to inbound marketing, especially in global business.

As president of Rapport International, a language services company that specializes in high-quality multilingual communications, I have had the opportunity to speak with hundreds of companies and organizations that do business in more than one language. Over the years, I have spoken with new clients to clarify their goals, analyze their current processes, assess their technology needs, and explain the various levels of quality of translation. When a company wants to grow and expand across borders or languages, understanding and implementing best practices is key to a successful journey. In this book, I share real-life stories and situations so that you can build a successful plan for international expansion. It starts with your global marketing. I then touch upon the other areas that will need high-quality language services, like legal, accounting, and technical. But in this book, I start with marketing since that is where the journey begins.

I encourage you to reach out to me, "Wendy Pease Translation Expert," on LinkedIn (www.linkedin.com/in/wendypease/). I am very active on that platform, and post language and culture information daily to "edutain" (educate and entertain). I encourage you to share any fun new information with me.

BREAKING BARRIERS

As a child, I learned that a warm smile opens some doors but is no substitute for engaging people in conversation, particularly when you want to do business with them. In international marketing, high-quality translation is imperative for connecting you with your buyers and bringing them through their journey to a completed sale. Having materials that are in the right language and culturally appropriate for your target audience will bring you greater success.

We are often contacted by "accidental exporters"—companies with good websites that attract international clients. The smart professionals at these companies call us to talk about translating their website to increase outreach in the markets already showing an interest in their products or services. According to the marketing research firm Common Sense Advisory, over 90 percent of people who speak English as a second language want to read website content in their native language and over 56 percent will spend more on purchases from translated websites.[1] With good translation on your website, you have the potential to dramatically increase sales and profit.

One accidental exporter we work with is Numberall Stamp and Tool, a company founded in 1930 that manufactures metal-marking equipment for stamping serial numbers, date codes, product codes, and other forms of permanent identification. The sales department saw an increase in requests for information from Spanish speakers, so they wisely decided to have their website translated and contacted us for advice and translation. In addition to translating their website, we worked with them to set up an automatic alert any time Numberall posted a blog. When we got the alert, we translated and uploaded the Spanish blog to their site. The addition of Spanish content to their website increased their revenue in previously untapped markets.

HOW MUCH ADDITIONAL REVENUE ARE YOU PASSING UP?

Defined simply, outbound marketing consists of traditional sales activities: Developing leads for outreach, cold calling, sending direct mail/email, and networking. Alternatively, inbound marketing consists of providing helpful online content so your buyer can find you and research your offerings prior to direct contact. With a defined inbound strategy, well-written content, and social media outreach, you can bring qualified leads *to you* instead of continually searching for new leads. You can become an exporter by thoughtfully developing a global inbound marketing plan.

The opportunity for global inbound marketing is huge! Less than 1 percent of the 30 million US companies export, and of those, 98 percent are small and mid-sized businesses (having fewer than 500 employees).[2] Moreover, businesses that export perform better. They have:

- Higher revenues.

- More profit (over 15 percent).

- Smoother business cycles.

- More efficient production capabilities.

- Stronger position in their domestic markets.

- Intellectual property value increases.

- Higher overall business value.

Exporters come from all industries—manufacturing, consulting, accounting, consumer products, food and beverage, marketing services, medical devices, electronics, and so many more.[3] It is no surprise that companies that already export tend to have a leader who has international experience and/or a curiosity about the world, rather than a product or service that is guaranteed to succeed but with a few exceptions—like health clubs, restaurants, dry cleaners, and hair salons—companies that do not export are missing big opportunities.

Knowledge eliminates fear and offers tools for success. When the world shut down for COVID-19, organizations that relied solely on outbound tactics to build sales suddenly struggled. Those businesses that quickly transitioned to inbound and online relationships recovered faster. We also saw how connected we are in the world today—within months, the disease spread around the world.

With good global marketing practices, you can grow the reach and strength of your company. The importance of the global market cannot be overlooked by any business leader that expects to be successful.

In this book, in addition to exploring the global opportunity and expanding upon global inbound, I will discuss how to build a strategy, what to know about technology and multilingual communications, what processes work best, how to translate your marketing content, and how to avoid pitfalls and use best practices. After you understand the foundational concepts, I will point out special considerations on handling incoming business, bringing people to your website, connecting across cultures, and the importance of diversity and inclusion.

By the end of the book, you will understand inbound terminology and have a road map for how to launch into new markets. My goal is to show marketing experts, creative agency advisors, business owners, and leadership coaches a way to build a plan, have a process, and connect with resources to effectively use inbound principals to market internationally.

Along the way, I share fun translation mistakes, cultural gaffes, and plenty of real stories.

Visit us at www.RapportTranslations.com for free bonus content and additional fun global marketing material.

@wendypease

www.linkedin.com/in/wendypease/

www.facebook.com/wendypease

www.instagram.com/wendy.pease

www.wendypease.com

www.RapportTranslations.com

Clubhouse @WendyPease

CHAPTER 1

BIG OR SMALL, ANY COMPANY CAN GO GLOBAL

"Use your fear...it can take you to the place where you store your courage."
—*Amelia Earhart*

When we lived in Taiwan, we loved getting Frosted Flakes. We had to go to a small, dimly lit, back-alley store. If we got lucky, they had cereal of some kind. Really lucky meant finding Frosted Flakes! It depended on the flow of black-market goods. Fast-forward to today, people in many parts of the world can order Frosted Flakes for delivery. Kellogg's is a large company and has the resources to export internationally. But what do you do if you are not as big as Kellogg's and want to grow your business into the global market?

Historically, companies had to have a plan, contacts, money, experience, connections—the list goes on.

Due to those onerous prerequisites, only 1 percent of US small businesses reached into the global market for fresh growth, leaving a lot of markets untapped. And of that 1 percent, only 2 percent of businesses export to more than one country, with Canada and Mexico being the most frequent countries among US exporters.[4]

Yet, the situation is changing. No longer is it just Frosted Flakes and products from large companies selling globally. Now, smaller consumer product companies and manufacturers are having great success.

What changed? *Everything.* The internet opened global markets and global disposable income increased. American products are in demand around the world. Non-US consumers frequently buy from companies outside their home country. Traveling internationally is easier, and millennials, with their large appetite for spending on experiences, embrace different languages and cultures.

If your company is not looking to sell globally, you are missing out on a *huge* opportunity!

Let us look at some encouraging statistics:

- By 2021, global retail e-commerce sales will reach $4.5 trillion.[5]

- 90 percent of searchers have not made their mind up about a brand before starting their search.[6]

- 87 percent of US shoppers begin product searches on digital channels.[7]

Consider the fact that companies are becoming accidental exporters in this climate. They create a website and get orders online from other countries without having to develop a plan! Astute marketers track that information and then target others who match their ideal marketing persona in those countries.

Perhaps it is time to tap into the global market and give your company a competitive advantage. Here are a few companies that did, and they are not looking back.

Bassetts Ice Cream of Philadelphia (the US Small Business Association (SBA) 2012 National Exporter of the Year) jumped into the world market in 2008, a long time after its founder, Lewis Bassett, originally began producing and selling the product from his New Jersey farm in 1861. Since then, Bassetts (the oldest ice cream manufacturer in the US) has found an excited base of fans in China as well as in the Bahamas and Anguilla. Thanks to exporting, the company is well on its way towards becoming an international brand. Sales are up, and future opportunities to expand abound. No longer does the company have to rely solely on a strong American economy to survive.[8]

Rekluse, an American manufacturer of performance clutch components for motorcycles, had an overseas market from the day it opened in 2002.

By working with the SBA to create a solid global marketing plan, the company saw a significant rise in sales from 2011–2012, when the company's export footprint expanded from 34 countries to 42. In the first quarter of 2012, the company's international sales rose 52 percent and propelled them into a new period of growth that required a 40 percent increase in employees. Now, more than 30 percent of the company's total revenue comes from international sales.[9]

Products are not the only goods in demand. Foreign buyers want services from US companies too.

According to CNN Business in 2019:

"Services are the biggest US export, with total foreign sales of $778 billion last year. Indeed, the United States has a $243 billion trade surplus in services, which is good news since service industries account for 71% of US jobs."[10]

Service industries that have big global reach include:[11]

- Travel and transportation: $236 billion.

- Finance and insurance: $76 billion.

- Sales from intellectual property, which includes software, movies, and television shows: $49 billion.

At Rapport International, we see US marketing companies doing more international work for two reasons:1) their clients expand across countries and ask for service; 2) importers want creative agencies in the US that understand the "American culture." A lot of that spending is for digital advertising. Digital advertising (internet ads) continues to increase and become more of the total ad spend. In 2019, global digital advertising spending was $333 billion, and for the first time it surpassed 50 percent of the total global advertising spend of $586 billion.[12]

Now, let's examine more numbers to quantify the opportunity.

TOTAL GLOBAL POPULATION

The global population is approximately 7.8 billion. Around 326 million people live in the United States, which is only 4 percent of the world's population. In pure numbers, it is a very small proportion. Plus, that percentage is expected to drop in the future as the US has slower population growth compared to other countries.[13]

EXPECTED POPULATION CHANGES

In North America, immigration from the rest of the world is expected to be the primary driver of continued population growth. The US is expected to see a net increase of 85 million people due to immigration over the next 80 years. Meanwhile, in Canada, deaths are expected to outnumber births; immigrants also will be the source of Canadian population growth. The fastest growing countries will be outside of North America. By 2100, experts expect African countries will lead the population growth.[14]

If we look at the following table from Pew Research Center, we can see that the largest countries by population changed over time. In the1950s, big countries beyond the top four included Japan, Germany, the UK, and Italy. Fast-forward to 2020 and China, India, and the US still top the list, but Japan and the European countries drop off the list, with Indonesia, Pakistan, Brazil, and Mexico replacing them.

By 2100, five of the world's 10 largest countries are projected to be in Africa

Countries with largest population, in millions

1950		2020		2100	
China	554	China	1,439	India	1,450
India	376	India	1,380	China	1,065
U.S.	159	U.S.	331	Nigeria	733
Russia	103	Indonesia	274	U.S.	434
Japan	83	Pakistan	221	Pakistan	403
Germany	70	Brazil	213	D.R. Congo	362
Indonesia	70	Nigeria	206	Indonesia	321
Brazil	54	Bangladesh	165	Ethiopia	294
UK	51	Russia	146	Tanzania	286
Italy	47	Mexico	129	Egypt	225

Note: Countries are based on current borders. In this data source, China does not include Hong Kong, Macau or Taiwan.
Source: United Nations Department of Economic and Social Affairs, Population Division, "World Population Prospects 2019."

PEW RESEARCH CENTER

FASTEST GROWING ECONOMIES

Although measuring population growth is useful, big populations do not necessarily reflect big economies. No matter how many people there are, they must have money to buy your goods. Targeting large populations does not help you if people cannot push the "purchase" button.

Nasdaq outlined the fastest growing economies as of October 2020: Guyana, South Sudan, Bangladesh, Egypt, and Benin.[15] Measuring economic growth does not tell us everything we need to know, however. We could look at gross domestic product (GDP) to check the health of a country's economy but that just looks at the total national income. It does not consider how much it costs to live in that country and how the wealth is distributed among the people.

To make informed marketing decisions, you cannot directly compare average incomes across currencies since the cost of buying "stuff" varies. Rather than looking at average incomes in different countries, it makes more sense to look at purchasing power parity (PPP), which measures the ability of people to buy similar items.[16] For example, you need a lot less money in India in pure dollars to live a comparable lifestyle in the US. This gives us a more accurate view of the monetary impact in the country.

The following chart is an example of PPP, taken from Numbeo.[17] Look at the currency-adjusted prices for grocery items in the US compared to India:

Item	US price in dollars	India price in dollars
Chicken fillets, 1 lb.	$4.12	$1.43
Eggs, 1 dozen	$2.33	$0.90
Bread	$2.47	$0.42
Rice, 1 lb.	$1.82	$0.32
Tomatoes, 1 lb.	$1.94	$0.23

Your weekly grocery bill in India is substantially less than the cost of buying the same items in the US, so the income necessary to live an American-type lifestyle in India is lower. PPP looks at the relative purchasing power between countries but does not account for salaries, poverty levels, and other economic conditions of a country.

Understanding the comparative effects of purchasing power, let's look at PPP from 1950–2100 for the top 10 countries.[18] As you can see, the US drops in PPP over time. This means that people in the US will spend relatively more to live the same lifestyle. The countries in bold indicate the high-growth countries of each time-period in terms of populations.

1950	2020	2100 Projected
US	**China**	India
Russia	US	China
UK	**India**	US
Germany	Japan	**Indonesia**
India	Germany	Brazil
France	**Russia**	Philippines
China	Indonesia	Turkey
Italy	**Brazil**	**Nigeria**
Japan	UK	Japan
Canada	France	Russia

What do we notice across time? Economies change. We can easily see that in the 1950s, the hot areas for international trade for the US included Europe, with the rebuilding of Germany (and Japan) after WWII. Looking at 2020, the hot countries for trade over the last decade are Brazil, Russia, India, and China—known as the BRIC countries in economic circles.

Projecting to 2100, some newcomers make the list. Notice how Indonesia and Nigeria are on the growing population list *and* the projected PPP list. Experts expect them to become hot markets.

Now, let's look at the numbers in a different way because growth and PPP only tell us so much.

DISPOSABLE INCOME

With PPP, you are measuring what people are able to buy across currencies. Disposable income tells us how much "extra" money people have. Disposable income is the remainder available for savings and spending on vacations, entertainment, fun, and other extras after necessary expenses such as mortgage/rent payments, groceries, health insurance, and taxes in a typical year. Have you ever calculated your disposable income? The formula is:

$$\text{Income - necessities = disposable income}$$

So, if your company sells consumer products or services that might be considered "extra," it is worth targeting places where residents with higher disposable income can afford your products.

The countries with the highest disposable income as of April 2020:[19]

1. United States $53k

2. Luxembourg $47k

3. Switzerland $42k

4. Germany $41k

5. Australia $40k

6. Norway $39.5k

7. Austria $38k

8. Belgium $36k

9. Netherlands $35.9k

10. Canada $35.7k

As we know, countries and incomes are not stable across time. If we look for countries with growing disposable incomes, the list changes. As of 2018, the countries with the highest annual *growth* in disposable income are:[20]

1. Costa Rica 7.4%

2. Latvia 6.6%

3. Czech Republic 4.7%

4. New Zealand 4.6%

5. Ireland 4.4%

6. Hungary 4.3%

7. Estonia 3.7%

8. Slovenia 3.7%

9. Canada 3.6%

10. Luxembourg 3.3%

The US ranks number 15 on this list. The US market has high disposable income per capita, yet on growth rates of disposable income and PPP, other markets look better.

WHAT DO THE NUMBERS MEAN?

The world is changing, opportunities abound outside US borders, and companies that recognize this trend will have bigger growth, hire more people, and experience greater success. With a logical process, support systems, and commitment, your organization can seize this opportunity.

According to the US Department of Commerce, companies that export are more successful. Remember the statistics from the Introduction of this book? Research shows that exporting makes you bigger, faster, smoother, and stronger.[21]

THE US GLOBAL MARKET: INCLUDE MULTILINGUAL MARKETING AT HOME

If we do not talk about multilingual marketing in the US, we would be missing key information about opportunities close to home.

Before my family moved to Taiwan, we lived in Mexico City, where I attended a school that did half a day in Spanish and the other half in English. By second grade, I knew the difference between the languages, whereas my younger brothers, who were in preschool, used both languages as one. My mom would try to use them as interpreters because they could understand things she could not. She would ask them what someone at the door said and they would just look at her. They could not understand why she did not know. They knew what language to speak to the Spanish speaking preschool teachers and what language to speak to Mom, yet they could not have told you what language they were speaking.

When we moved back to the United States, some of the children laughed when my brothers spoke. They would say "speak some more like that," meaning "speak Spanish." Of course, very quickly the young children stopped speaking Spanish. In those days, when immigrants came to the US, they "melted" into the pot by trying to assimilate and learn English without an accent. It was odd to see foreign language speakers outside their homes.

These days, it is different. Immigrants come to the US and retain their language and heritage. Rather than calling the US a "melting pot," I have heard it called a "mixed salad"—a dish that relishes the differences of flavors, textures, and colors. And this mix adds value to our society: just think of tacos, enchiladas, samosas, moo shu pork, pho noodles, sushi, and pizza.[22]

The US multilingual market offers a huge opportunity. Let's look at the US Spanish-speaking market alone.

The US has the second largest population of Spanish speakers in the world, second only to Mexico! The size of the Spanish speaking market in the US is close to 40 million people. This population is larger than that of Peru, Venezuela, Chile, Ecuador, Guatemala, Cuba, Honduras, and many other countries.[23]

Additionally, the Hispanic population growth in the US outpaces the growth of every other group, and that expansion is expected to be a continuing trend. Granted, not all Latinos in the US speak Spanish, yet many do and continue to speak Spanish at home, even if they are second or third generation. Therefore, the opportunity for capturing the Hispanic market increases when you provide marketing translation into the Spanish language.[24]

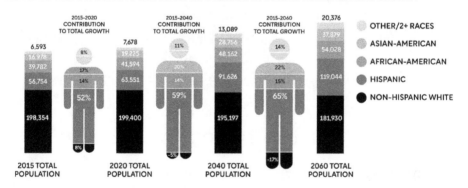

HISPANIC POPULATION WILL CONTUNUE TO RISE; NON-HISPANIC WHITE POPULATION WILL CONTINUE TO DECLINE

HISPANICS WILL CONTINUE TO ACCOUNT FOR OVER 50% OF FUTURE U.S. POPULATION GROWTH

Source: U.S. Census Bureau, 2014 National Population Projections

Plus, the younger generation of Hispanics often retains their language and culture even when born in the US. The number of Latino millennials who identify as bilingual is growing dramatically in the US, Nielsen reports. Additionally, 62 percent of the country's adult Latinos speak English or are bilingual, according to Pew Research Center's National Survey of Latinos.[25]

Considering the preference of consumers for companies to provide information in their native language (more on this later in Chapter 4), US companies that do not provide marketing content and advertisements in Spanish are likely missing out on more than 40 million potential customers and counting.

In October 2016, Facebook released the results of their Facebook IQ study conducted by Latinum Network. The researchers studied 500 Hispanics from different backgrounds of language usage: English-dominant, bilingual, and Spanish-dominant.

The study[26] had several conclusions, including:

- Ads targeting Hispanics in Spanish significantly increase their interest in purchasing products.

- When online, more than 80 percent of Spanish-dominant Hispanics use Spanish at least half of the time when they read, write, or watch videos.

- 79 percent of Spanish-dominant, 82 percent of bilingual, and 60 percent of English-dominant Hispanics surveyed think brands should reach out to consumers in both English and Spanish.

- 58 percent of Spanish-dominant Hispanics and 48 percent of bilingual Hispanics think that the brands that reach out in Spanish demonstrate they value the Hispanic community.

Just think about the potential for increasing inbound marketing! By translating your website into Spanish, you have the potential to reach the Spanish-speaking residents in the US, Mexico, and all other Spanish-speaking countries around the world.

JOIN THE PROS

Many companies already know the value of advertising to Spanish speakers on television.

To check out some popular advertisements, visit our blog about Spanish advertisements in the US: www.rapporttranslations.com/blog/spanish-advertisements-in-the-us-fuel-for-sales-growth.

In the blog, you can watch advertisements by Crest, Dodge, Carl's Jr., Chevy, Target, Subway, and more well-known companies that advertise in

Spanish to win new customers in the US.

Yes, those brands are consumer products, and you might think that business-to-business services need not consider Spanish marketing. But US Hispanics are ahead of the curve when it comes to digital as they lead in adoption of new devices, are power users of mobile, and over-index in video consumption.[27] Think about the opportunity to reach a market this connected!

To give you an idea of the potential scale, Procter & Gamble Co. spent $369 million in Hispanic media in 2017 alone. Think about *your* products or services. Might there be ways that you can reach out to this market to increase your growth close to home? To read more about the opportunity you can visit *Ad Age*'s Hispanic Fact Pack.[28]

CONCLUSION

All the numbers, analysis, and research show that exporters are more successful. Organizations that take the risk to expand globally benefit in so many ways. Of course, conducting business on a global scale is not without challenges, but thanks to improvements in trade finance, the internet, and trade agreements that are helping to balance trade deficits, exporting has never been easier. Agencies like the US Small Business Association provide exporting counselors and resource partners that are ready and willing to help your company make the global leap. Looking at this opportunity, can you still find an excuse for *not* exporting? With the useful and simple instructions in this book, you can learn how to benefit from reaching the Global Market.

ACTION STEPS:

1. Do a readiness assessment of your company for multilingual marketing. Is your senior leadership on board with expanding to non–English-speaking markets?

2. Evaluate your English inbound marketing and what might need to be improved upon for better success.

3. Research and pick one non-English-speaking market to target.

4. Contact the local trade expert near you and learn about the support they offer. Find your State Export center and the SBA contact at this website: 2016.export.gov/eac/.

CHAPTER 2

ALIGN INTERNALLY FOR A SUCCESSFUL EXPANSION

"Alone we can do so little, together we can do so much."
—*Helen Keller*

After more than 15 years in the language-translation business, I have heard a variety of reasons why companies start exporting or adopting multilingual marketing. Rarely does it start with a well-thought-out strategy based on goals. That is fine…if it works. What is not fine is continuing to export or incorporate multilingual marketing with a "ready, fire, aim" process. I see more success with companies that do have a clearly defined strategy and goal.

Recently, I spoke with a prospective client that had one person in charge of procuring translation services but the process for every language varied. Only she knew where to send internal clients for each language's translation: the local market representative, a specific agency for certain languages, individual translators, or internal employees for other languages. Standard guidelines for brand messaging, consistency, or quality control were nonexistent. If that one individual got hit by a proverbial bus, the company had no way to recreate the system. Surprisingly, the company is a large, successful business, which grew internationally because its clients with global work wanted multilingual services.

Here are some of the reasons that companies start global marketing:

1. **Random opportunity:** A chance meeting at a conference or a fortuitous connection from networking unearths an opportunity in another country not previously considered.

2. **Increasing sales:** These days, it is common for companies to be found on the internet and win orders or clients from online searches. Paying attention and responding to buying signals creates accidental exporters.

3. **Owner wants to travel:** Adventurous owners who like to travel identify countries that they like and look for business opportunities to allow for more "business trips." It is fun to mix personal/ business travel; expanding internationally gives a great opportunity to do so.

4. **Owner is from another country:** "New Americans" from other countries are more likely to export to their own country and/or be open to other cultures. They have less fear of cross-border or cross-language business.

5. **Current clients:** Companies that get requests from clients are willing to explore new opportunities to retain clients. It is a common way to start exporting.

6. **Legal or regulatory requirements:** By law, governments, schools, and medical providers must provide in-language communications to the people they serve. If a life sciences company sells into France, the company must meet the European Union regulations. In Canada, bilingual English and French labeling is required.

7. **Competitive move:** Sometimes, companies will see competitors expanding internationally and jump on the bandwagon.

8. **Internal champion:** Recently, we spoke with a new vice president, who was hired to grow sales and marketing at his company. He had worked internationally before, so he understood the potential and the process of building an international organization. He became the internal champion, educating the senior leadership team.

9. **Located near Canada or Mexico:** Companies located near the borders find demand for their products. It is easy to transport and fill these needs. They become exporters while working locally.

10. **Partnering with global contacts:** Lawyers, for example, often have relationships with firms in other countries, so that when clients have international needs, the firm already has in-country experts. We have seen such synchronization across creative firms, logistics companies, printers, distributors, and manufacturers. From their international interactions, the leaders gain experience and begin business in new countries.

You might relate to one if not more of those reasons. Rarely do we see someone say, "I am going to start exporting and I have a strategic plan." Yet, to be successful, creating a strategy is a smart step. If you are leading or working for a growing company that decides to focus on international expansion or US expansion to multilingual markets, you know your goal. But you might wonder about how to create a strategy. My biggest suggestion is to make sure that your multilingual strategy aligns with your corporate strategy and marketing strategy overall. Here are a few suggestions on how to align your expansion plans with corporate and marketing goals and to control your communications so that they remain appropriate.

KNOW YOUR CORPORATE STRATEGY TO MAKE INFORMED DECISIONS

You need to look at your company's overall strategy to understand the vision, mission, values, goals, and objectives before you start translating your website and other marketing materials in hopes of reaching a new target audience. If you do not understand your corporate strategy, you will waste time figuring out your priorities, whether they are languages, materials, client support, or any other questions coming your way.

If you do not have a company strategy, start there. If you do not know if your company has one, find out. If you have been asked to handle translation, find out if guidance exists on what should be translated so that you are not wasting time and money on unnecessary translations.

At a minimum, a company's strategy should include a vision, mission, and value statements as well as clearly defined goals and objectives. Objectives and goals change, so I will provide general examples. If you want more information on building a company strategy, a good book to read is *Traction* by Gino Wickman. He gives a clearly defined roadmap on how to set a direction for your company.

Below I define the terms to include in a strategy and give Rapport International's mission, vision, and values as examples.

Vision is the big, pie-in-the-sky view of what you are trying to accomplish. Our company vision is: "Connecting people for a peaceful and prosperous world."

Mission is what you focus on daily. Our mission is: "To unite people across language and culture."

Values are the guiding principles around which the team rallies. Ours include:

- Connect: with each other, our clients, our linguists, no matter the language or culture.

- Understand: truly "get" what our clients want and what each person says.

- Deliver: results count. Our focus is on delivering accurate results, on time, and on budget.

- Quality: we focus on quality so that people depend on us.

Everything that we do in our language services company follows those guiding principles to make decisions. We focus on building "rapport" in our relationships and delivering quality. That hallmark is our positioning, yet other companies in the industry have different orientations.

One competitor focuses on being cheap and accessible. They crowd-source translations, which are done by whoever is available. It is done fast and inexpensively; their target customer wants to save money and time. They are not as worried about confidentiality or ownership of the material.

Another competitor focuses on machine translation. They process large quantities of text or data into a "gist" translation. It gives a general idea of what the content is so that the client can narrow down the exact content they want to submit for a quality translation. We see law firms use this method to find the content that they want to use for a legal exhibit. Then, the lawyer can pay for a quality translation for just the parts they need.

You can imagine that each of these companies would have very different strategy documents.

Once you have your vision, mission, and values, the direction becomes obvious. The next step is to break down what you need to do to establish the attainable steps. It is good to have a 10-year vision, three- to five-year goals, and then get to your one-year action plan.

Goals: The old saying is, "You need to know where you are going in order to get there." Goals define what you want to accomplish and outline clear objectives to reach your goals. A goal could be to increase revenues. Successful companies set long-term goals in three-year time spans and break those down into annual and then quarterly goals. For example, at Rapport International, we deliver excellent service, yet we realized we did not do a good job of building relationships with clients; we did not create an "experience," which meant that when our contact left the company, we would not hear about their departure even if they were a loyal and satisfied client. We provided excellent services but had not developed a strong enough relationship for them to tell us when they were leaving the company. Nor would we hear about upcoming changes like new market openings, new partnerships, or current challenges that could affect us. At our annual meeting, we set a three-year goal to deepen relationships with our clients. In year one, we set goals to identify our VIP clients, visit those clients in person to build relationships, increase outgoing phone calls, send handwritten cards, and ask more questions about what clients want. For each quarter, we clarified metrics and activities around each goal. We are in the middle of the three-year goal, yet already we can see a difference in relationships and continuity of business.

Objectives: Using the SMART acronym, our objectives are specific, measurable, actionable, realistic, and time bound. By setting objectives, leaders define exactly how the company is going to reach the goals. For example, for our client experience goal, we set an objective for our team member in Nebraska to visit two clients per week. That objective tells him what to do, when, and how many times per week. This meets the SMART criteria.

Once you set the company strategy, then the marketing team can develop a marketing strategy to align with the corporate goals. When all the teams work together towards the company strategy, the company will get where you want it to go.

The strategy for expanding into new markets should define:

- What you are trying to achieve.
- How to allocate resources.
- What the budget is.
- What you will be focusing on and talking about as a company.

Defining those points will help align everyone with both your corporate strategy and what the goals are for the new target markets.

ALIGN THE MARKETING STRATEGY AND CREATE A MARKETING PLAN FOR EXPANSION

Once the company direction is set, each department sets goals and objectives to support the corporate strategy.

The marketing strategy defines the specific audience (or persona), the key benefits, and the right time to capture the attention of the audience most likely to be interested in your product or service. By defining the marketing strategy, the company can then develop a plan with actionable goals.

Once you know your strategy, it is time to develop a marketing plan, which includes your strategy, goals, situation analysis, and SWOT (strengths, weaknesses, opportunities, threats) analysis. The first time you build the plan, it will take a while, but it will get easier each year you update it because you have already laid the groundwork.

As this book's focus is on global growth, I want to spend most of our time on the specifics of that. However, if you have not built a strong foundation, it will be harder to achieve your global goals. If you are not familiar with building a marketing plan, you can search the internet for many resources on how to do it for your company.

Inbound Back Office and Acorn30 are marketing services agencies.

Company	Inbound Back Office	Acorn30
Customer	marketing agencies, consultants, and HubSpot partner agencies	manufacturers and agriculture businesses
Competitors – direct and indirect	other marketing staffing firms, internal hires, independent contractors	other inbound growth companies and marketing agencies
Product/Services offered	expert marketing support for marketing agencies, consultants, and HubSpot partner agencies	strategy, websites, lead generation, inbound, HubSpot resellers, content marketing
Place (Location)	US – IN based	US and Canada – Canada based
Promotion	networking with partners, direct outreach	inbound marketing, networking, direct sales
Price	hourly	project fees or retainer

Typical marketing plans include more detail on the preceding categories. Professional marketers call the practice the "three Cs" (company, customer, competitors) and "four Ps" (product, place, promotion, price) framework. You can see that both companies are marketing agencies with HubSpot expertise that sell inbound and growth services, but they provide different services and target different customers. How they talk to their target personas, what content they write, where they spend their time, and how they use visuals will, therefore, be quite different. Once you understand your approach, the next step is to create a marketing plan for the year that supports the corporate and marketing strategies. If the corporate strategy is to launch in foreign-speaking markets, you need to figure out what steps the marketing department needs to take to accomplish those goals. A well-developed marketing plan will address those areas.

In addition to the three Cs and four Ps, marketing plans include a SWOT analysis. The table below shows a sample SWOT analysis from a HubSpot Partner agency that focuses on technology companies in the Boston area.

Strengths (INTERNAL)	Weaknesses (INTERNAL)
• Great strategists and content writers • Creative office environment • Known in local tech market for strategy work • Fully staffed	• Technical skills are weak • Business development not strong • Rent increasing • Lack of internal HR growth plan
Opportunities (EXTERNAL)	**Threats (EXTERNAL)**
• Speaking opportunities • Biotech industry growing locally • Increasing inbound leads • Partner to increase tech skills • Leverage good content writers • New markets	• Competitors hiring trained staff • Uncertain economy • Lots of HubSpot agencies

By taking the time to create a marketing plan, you start to see patterns of places where your company can grow and where you want to focus your energy. Many companies try to jump to answer questions like:

- How much content should we create this year?
- Where should we advertise?
- Shall we make a brochure or redo our website?
- Should we go to that conference next month?
- How much should we spend on Facebook/Google/LinkedIn advertising?
- Should we translate our website?

It is virtually impossible to answer these questions logically without a marketing plan. It will take more time to guess answers than to take the time to write a marketing plan to answer these questions throughout the year.

Plus, your marketing plan will set metrics against which you can measure your progress so that you can adjust each subsequent year, leading to better planning and anticipating returns. With a clear plan, you can adapt it for your multilingual marketing.

It is good to remember that if you are going to test your marketing message or activities in English, the results will not necessarily carry over to other languages, so be sure to add enough time in your planning to test everything for each new target market. We will discuss this topic more later.

RECEIVING AN INQUIRY
FROM A NEW MARKET

The first thing to do when you get an inquiry from a customer in a new market is refer to your corporate strategy to decide what to do. Is the request from a market that is a strategic target for the company this year, or is it a singular request from somewhere that is not on the company's radar? The answer to those questions will help you decide whether you need to go to the expense of obtaining professional translation services to communicate with the new customer, if machine translation is enough for this one customer, or if you do not need to take any action.

If you get a request from a new customer in Germany, for example, refer to your corporate strategy before you decide to translate information into German. If you see that part of the strategic plan is to launch in Germany (or a new market), then pursuing translation services makes good business sense. If, on the other hand, you see that expansion in Germany is not part of the strategy and the focus is on launching in Peru, Argentina, and

Mexico, you have insight that helps you decide not to spend money on a German translation for this one customer. The Spanish-speaking market is where the company is going to spend its time, budget, and travel to support the corporate mission this year.

Of course, there are always outliers. For instance, if you are going to double your business because the German market suddenly opened, then it might make sense to reassess. In this case, you will still need to make sure the corporate executives are in alignment with any new goals before making any decisions.

In any case, when you get those types of calls and requests, you need to step back and make an informed decision based on corporate goals and strategies rather than have the person in charge of translation or marketing communications decide whether it is in the budget.

The strategy for expanding into new markets is a section in your marketing plan and defines:

- Company goals

- Resource allocation

- Budget

- Expected outcomes

Those factors align everyone with your corporate strategy and what the goals are for the new target markets.

BEST PRACTICES FOR EXPANSION INTO MULTILINGUAL MARKETS

To maximize your company's chances of success in new foreign-language markets, this book will give you all the information you need. Or you could bring in a multilingual marketing expert right from the start. Your translation service provider should specialize in marketing translation and work tightly with your marketing department in planning and implementing your strategy. They can provide expertise, guide you toward measurable, realistic goals, suggest services that will support those goals, and create a Translation Management Plan to define the steps to reach your company goals.

The companies that I have seen obtain the greatest success in new markets have partnered at some point with a multilingual expert who is involved in the strategic planning along with marketing so that translation is not an afterthought.

ACTION STEPS:

1. Start with your corporate strategy.

2. Bring in the people who have a stake in the plan—executives, marketing, and a multilingual marketing expert.

3. Assess your SWOT plan for risks and opportunities.

4. Assign a person or department to take ownership of the marketing in the new market.

5. Document how to move forward with your multilingual marketing.

6. Review and redo your annual goals and objectives.

Armed with those tips, you now have a great starting point for expanding into multilingual markets. The next chapters take a deeper look into each aspect of global inbound, starting with the basics—technology advances, quality considerations, pitfalls to watch out for, and how to build an affordable process for your communications needs.

CHAPTER 3

GLOBAL MARKETING BASICS

"Don't Push people to where you want to be; meet them where they are."
—*Meghan Keaney Anderson, former VP of Marketing for HubSpot*

I n the language field, there is a big difference between a translator and an interpreter. A translator works with written materials. Typically, a translator likes a quiet space to work and write and can quote dictionaries, whereas an interpreter likes to talk and be around people. An interpreter facilitates spoken communication between people—either in person, on the phone, or through a video call.

When a client calls for a translator, we talk about the project so that I know whether to assign a translator or interpreter. I listen carefully to the caller to find out whether they understand the basic terminology for what they are asking. One of my missions in life is to educate people about the difference between the meaning of the words, "translation" and "interpretation." Using the right terminology will help you get what you need faster.

As you become more involved in global marketing you will hear the words "globalization," "localization," "transcreation," "transliteration," and more. These are more specific industry terms that fall under the category of translation. In this book and when speaking to clients, I use the word "translation" to keep it simple, yet I silently understand when they need localization, globalization, or any other specific service.

For definitions of other terminology, visit the glossary at the end of the book, where I explain the terms as I use them and for specific industry meaning.

EXPORTING CONSIDERATIONS

As you start your global marketing journey, there are other functional areas that need to travel with you. I will touch on the subjects but not go in depth since an entire book could be written about each topic. Moreover, I am not an expert in these areas. Instead, I have included and recommend topics and sources for you to consider as you start your global inbound journey in the Resources section.

Legal: As with any venture, you want to make sure you have a clear legal contract with any partner you engage in business. Laws differ between countries so a standard US legal agreement might not suffice. In picking a lawyer, make sure to hire one with international experience or find a firm that has legal partners in your targeted countries. If you decide to translate any agreements, make sure your contract identifies which language prevails in case a legal or language interpretation dispute arises.

Accounting: If you continue to work from one office in the US and ship internationally, you might not have additional taxes. If you hire a salesperson or distributor in another country, you might have to pay that country's local taxes. Again, find an accountant who does international work or has partner offices.

Shipping company: Companies specialize in different packages, geographies, and expertise. If your product has constraints (see below) or requirements, it is worth finding a fit.

ITAR: ITAR (International Traffic in Arms Regulations) is a US regulation to control the export of defense and military related technologies to safeguard US national security. Obviously, if you sell guns, weapons, or products that endanger the US, you will have many restrictions. If you sell parts that may be used to make any regulated item, you are also subject to ITAR regulations. Some manufacturing technologies, programming in warfare-gaming systems, transporting a computer internationally with protected information, or sharing a network with protected information with a non-approved person while they are in the US are examples of ITAR violations.

In-country representatives: Once you establish consistent sales, you might need a business presence on the ground. However, that does not mean you have to hire an employee. You have options to start slowly and build. You can hire an international professional employer organization

(PEO), subcontract to a company to act as a company representative, partner with a distributor, partner with another business owner, or contract with another company already selling in the country. As relationships are considered more important in other parts of the world than in the US (more on that topic in Chapter 19), I highly recommend traveling to the country and meeting with potential partners prior to making any deal. Take your time to find the right person, as breaking off a business relationship can be difficult—financially, emotionally, and legally.

Bribes: Oh, this question is a big one. Cultures around the world define bribes differently. All compliance people at large companies take a hard stance against bribes: Absolutely NO bribes are allowed. I was in the audience when a panel of compliance people spoke, and it was a boring panel. How many ways can four people say, "No bribes allowed"? Yet, if we could get a US in-country businessperson in a private room, the stories would be different. Not because the businesspeople are unethical but because bribes are defined differently. For example, is slipping a $20 to a maître d' to get a better table at a fine restaurant a bribe? Is bringing flowers to a receptionist to sweeten her up to let you talk to the CEO a bribe? Is paying cash to a government official for taxes a bribe? Is giving cash to a police officer to stay out of jail for an uncommitted offense a bribe? Is it a bribe when your best friend's company sends business to your firm or receives business from your firm instead of one of the other companies in the bidding process? Well, it depends. We all know that bribes are bad, yet culturally, you will find gray zones amongst countries on what is a bribe and what is an expected business practice. Make sure you understand your personal beliefs, country expectations, laws, and your company's regulations fully before crossing into any gray zone.

SUPPORT RESOURCES

A few months ago, we got a call from a technical solutions company as the owner got a State Trade Expansion Program (STEP) grant from the New Hampshire Office of International Commerce to translate his website. His company consults about safety and security operations at airports around the world. Even though most of his business is by referral for his specialized services, he realized that new clients expected him to have a website in their language. He needed it to add credibility and validity to his company. With the STEP grant, a new website, and high-quality translation from us, he has a nice looking and professionally translated website to connect with his clients. By making his site accessible in multiple languages, he can reach new clients and close deals faster.

There are resources available to support small and mid-sized companies looking to master the many moving parts of exporting because the US federal government wants to stimulate business growth and level the balance of trade by increasing exports. And if you run a small or mid-sized business, it is nice to know that you are in good company. In fact, according to the US Chamber of Commerce, 98 percent of US exporters are small and mid-sized companies.[29]

A trade expert once told me that the biggest fear of exporting is not being able to speak the language.

On top of the fear of language barriers, people believe that there is enough business here in the US without exporting. Yet, as discussed in Chapter 1, in research by the US Department of Commerce, companies that export are 17 percent more profitable than companies that do not.

With the advice from this book and the list of government agencies, programs, and grants that support exporters in the Resources section, you can build a plan to increase your global inbound marketing to reach international buyers and build the strength, growth, and profitability of your company.

Once you decide to export, start with state resources.

You can visit this site to see what is available in your state: www.rapport-translations.com/blog/us-small-business-association-step-grant-initiative.

Each US state has an export resource center with advisors, industry and country-specific trade shows, introductions to global connections, an International Trade Administration advisor, education seminars, conferences, webinars, and a list of companies and service providers in the local area. By starting there, you gain access to experienced advisors who want to help you.

Ask them about STEP grants, which aim to increase the number of small businesses that are exporting and to increase the value of exports for those small businesses that are currently exporting. It is funded in part by the SBA. With total federal funding over $60 million, they want to find companies to fund. The funds can be used for marketing, business development, trade shows, trade missions, and translation. Marketing translation can include websites, SEO, and targeted marketing to overseas audiences.

With free resources to help, grants to help fund your growth, and experienced experts to guide your way, do not put off building The Language of *your* Global Marketing!

Before we go any further, look at your website analytics to see if you already have business coming in from other countries, which will give you some idea of where you might be able to start.

ACTION STEPS:

1. Consider what other functional groups in your business might need translation when you successfully bring in prospects from other countries.

2. Look into STEP grants to see what you need to do to qualify.

3. Research whether any ITAR or exporting regulations control your products or services.

4. Discuss any fears that your team might have in exporting and talk about the concerns.

CHAPTER 4

GLOBAL ENGLISH

"If you talk to a man in a language he understands, that goes to his head. If you talk to him in his language, that goes to his heart."
—Nelson Mandela

ENGLISH IS NOT THE GLOBAL LANGUAGE

Do you watch the Olympics? I am glued to the TV during the summer and winter Olympics. I love the international stage and the competition by people who trained hard for years. I love the national spirit of the countries supporting their athletes and, most of all, I love the cross-cultural and language advertisements! I watch on both English- and Spanish-speaking TV so I can see how the advertisers adapt their advertisements to each language.

That starts me wondering about the French language. Have you ever wondered why French is the official Olympic language if the Olympics originated in Greece? It all traces back to Pierre de Coubertin, who revived the Olympic Games at the end of the nineteenth century when French was considered the language of diplomacy. Since April 1915, the International Olympic Committee's (IOC) headquarters have been in the French-speaking region of Switzerland. According to the Olympic Charter, French and English are official IOC languages, yet if a discrepancy between a French text and an English one occurs in any IOC document, the French text prevails, so French is *the* official Olympic language.[30]

Imagine saying to the Olympic officials that English is the global language and you only need to communicate in English. It's not going to happen. English is not the global language. In the next section, I discuss the languages of the world and language preferences of people.

LANGUAGES OF THE WORLD

There are over 7,000 languages identified in the world today.[31] Yet, almost half of the world population—43 percent, which is 3.2 billion people—speaks one of the top 10 languages as their native tongue.

When you look at the total number of both native and non-native speakers for the top languages in the world, an even clearer picture emerges regarding how the world communicates. Despite Chinese being the largest natively spoken language, English comes out on top with the greatest number of speakers worldwide because many countries focus on teaching English as a second language in school.

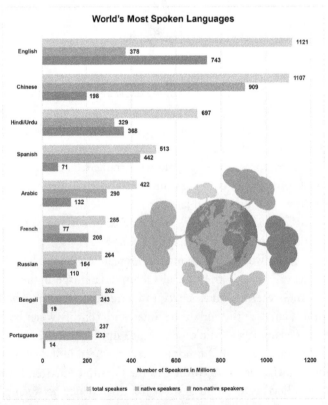

World's Most Spoken Languages

	total speakers	native speakers	non-native speakers
English	1121	378	743
Chinese	1107	909	198
Hindi/Urdu	697	329	368
Spanish	513	442	71
Arabic	422	290	132
French	285	77	208
Russian	264	154	110
Bengali	262	243	19
Portuguese	237	223	14

Number of Speakers in Millions

Source - https://blog.esl-languages.com/blog/learn-languages/most-spoken-languages-world/
January 15, 2019

Even though there are more Chinese and Spanish speakers than there are English speakers, the number of websites in English far outnumber websites in other languages.

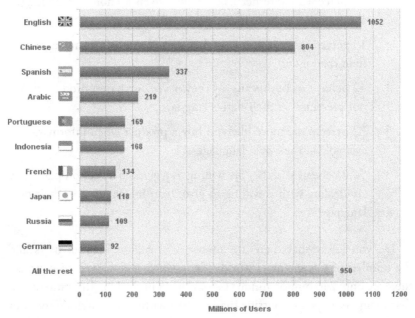

Top Ten Languages in the Internet in Millions of users - December 2017

Source: Internet World Stats - www.internetworldstats.com/stats7.htm
Estimated total Internet users are 4,156,932,140 in December 31, 2017
Copyright © 2018, Miniwatts Marketing Group

From the graphs, it looks like most internet users speak English—at least as a second language— and that most of the internet is in English. Therefore, it appears that it might be fine to keep all your content in English.

Here is more insight into that perspective.

Common Sense Advisory conducted a survey in eight countries and concluded that:[32]

- 72.1 percent of consumers spend time on websites written in their own language.

- 72.4 percent of consumers are more likely to buy a product if the label or information is in their own language.

- More than half of consumers are willing to pay more for products with information in their own language.

And Gallup[33] surveyed a group of internet users from the European Union and found that *less than half* of all respondents said they purchase products and services in languages other than their mother tongue. Look at these other statistics from the Gallup survey:

- 90 percent of internet users, when given a choice of languages, always visit a website in their own language.

- 19 percent of Europeans say they never browse in a language other than their own.

- 42 percent of Europeans say they never purchase a product that is not presented in their native language.

- 72 percent are more likely to buy a product when information is available in their own language.

- 56.2 percent said they are willing to pay more if the company they are dealing with is willing to give them information in their own language.

Do you know that there are almost 4.39 billion internet users and the number of Google users worldwide is *nearly four billion*? In contrast, there are only 246 million unique Google users in the US. This ratio means that many more people outside the US than within are searching for your products and services.[34]

Google holds 94 percent of the search market worldwide, so anyone around the world can find your electronic storefront, not just people in the US,[35] and Google provides its search ability in more than 130 languages. Think about it! Google's search engine knows that people want information and content in their native language but most companies are still providing information in English only. With a little strategy and planning, companies can develop multilingual websites to generate leads and connect with people in their native language. Trying to handle 130 languages from the start is overwhelming, and I would *not* recommend it. As you read through this book, you will develop a process to start with one foreign language, which can then be replicated to the other languages that make business sense for you.

If you offer content in about a dozen languages, you "speak" to over 75 percent of the world! What does that statistic tell us? While it is true that over one billion internet users in the world are English speakers (both native and non-native), there is a potential audience of 3.5 billion internet users out there who speak other languages. Additionally, only a fraction of those one billion English-speaking users are native speakers, and studies have shown that people prefer to visit websites that offer content in their native language. What that evidence all adds up to is that the world is full of potential leads, especially if you offer your products or services to them in their language.

WRITING IN GLOBAL ENGLISH

Even though English is not the global language, there are ways to write in "global English" to make sure your content translates your message clearly in other languages.

Ensure Your Written Content Is Precise: The best marketing translations typically come from copy with very precise language. Often English marketing materials have quite a bit of descriptive, elaborate language, which often does not translate well into different languages. Many languages need more words/symbols to convey the same meaning as an English document does. That effect can result in a confusing, overly long translation. To get the highest quality marketing translation, the best practice is for the English copy to be as precise and succinct as possible.

Finalize Copy Before Sending for Translation: Materials sent for translation should be the FINAL copy. If words are removed or changed from the English copy after the translation is complete, the alteration will not be captured. It is not just a matter of removing or changing the same words in the translation—it takes thought to make sure the message is consistent with the original language. Last-minute changes complicate the translation process in terms of keeping a clear message and accurate version control. To avoid such issues, always wait until the copy is final before sending it for marketing translation.

Consider BOTH Globalization and Localization: Globalization is a translation that can be used across different markets that understand the same language. Localization needs more adaptation. Some countries use a combination of both. For example, the McDonald's name and logo are consistent across many countries (globalized). When they chose to move into the fast-food market in India, McDonald's understood that their main product—beef—would not be culturally appropriate. McDonald's localized and moved into the India market with a new menu consisting of chicken, fish, and vegetarian options.

Avoid Humor and Tricky Grammar: Even within the US, what New Englanders find humorous might hit a flat note in Southern California. That likelihood also applies when translating humor to a new language and culture. I would recommend avoiding humor when marketing across countries and cultures. The same holds true when using tricky grammar, clever taglines, or commonly accepted categorizations. A former employee told me a story about the online discount shopping site Wish.com. They had an issue in 2016 with a marketing translation error that rendered what should have been "plus size" as "fat lady" on dozens of their offerings from their Chinese manufacturers. Social media became inundated with postings from offended customers, all pointing to Wish.com's inappropriate product titles. Even after explaining the error, negative feelings remained.[36] Such an error can irreparably harm a company's chances at success in a new market. Read Chapter 9 on quality to avoid similar situations.

Transcreate When Necessary: Transcreation goes one step beyond translation and not only translates the words and meaning but also adapts the entire message to the new culture and makes the message culturally appropriate to convey intent, style, tone, and context. Sometimes, transcreation will be the best option for your marketing translation.

For example, years ago, we received a letter originally written to target German CEOs. The company now wanted to target CEOs in the US. We translated the letter in its entirety, keeping the original meaning, but we kept hearing back from the client that it was not right. After speaking with the bilingual client, we understood he was looking for a "transcreation." He wanted us to adapt their letter for CEOs in the US without losing the essential message of the letter. Best practice in Germany to get the attention of CEOs is to write compliments and accolades in the beginning; however, a flowery introduction would not appeal to CEOs in the US as they prefer brief and to-the-point letters. Our client wanted us to rewrite the letter for their new target market. These days, we spend more time clarifying what a client wants at the start of the project.

Plan for Expansion: Remember that translating from one language into another is not as simple as changing each word in a document to the new language. Translation expands the written copy, and it can be 20 to 30 percent longer depending on the language. Expansion of copy that is overly descriptive or elaborate can result in a confusing translation, or in one that is overly long and will not fit into the allotted space on a document, manual, product package, presentation, graphic, or advertisement. To get the highest quality translation, having the original copy be as concise as possible is best. One of my favorite examples of expansion in translation is the word "fahrvergnugen," used by Volkswagen. This one German word when translated becomes four words in English: "The pleasure of driving." So, the client needed four times the number of words and 80 percent more type-space.

Use Repeat Copy Across Materials: Good marketers know that a potential client needs to hear a message seven to 10 times before the person "hears" the message. Therefore, using repeat copy across all your materials is a wise move and provides consistency in English and across other translated copy. Plus, if you use an experienced translation agency, they will probably use a translation memory tool, which keeps the translation content consistent and might reduce costs. A translation memory (TM) tool stores "segments" previously translated by a human expert. The project manager submits new documents to the TM tool, which matches segments and provides the previous translation to the linguist. It is not machine translation or artificial intelligence (AI) translation. It is a tool to keep your translations consistent. We will talk more about machine and AI translation in Chapter 7.

Advertising Should Be Culturally Appropriate: Whether you translate, globalize, or localize, visuals and pictures need to match the targeted region and culture. Models should be of the same race, locations should look like they belong to the region, and even colors should be culturally appropriate. For example, in Western cultures, the color white means purity, innocence, cleanliness, and goodness, and is worn by brides. In some Asian cultures, white symbolizes death, mourning, and bad luck, and is worn at funerals. I once saw a magazine back-page advertisement for car insurance with a lily-white family smiling broadly. It was a nice picture...except the ad was in the *Minority Business Magazine* (MBE). It would have been wiser to a show a family of color. Watch for similar mistakes on websites, in magazines, and in other promotional material. You would be surprised at how often such blunders happen.

Now that you understand that English is not *the* global language, you might be wondering, "How do I even start marketing internationally?" In the next chapter, I will give you some advice to answer this question.

ACTION STEPS:

1. Consider what language skills you might have in-house.

2. Think about language and cultural differences for your target countries.

3. Review your content to meet the guidelines discussed above.

CHAPTER 5

STARTING AND PLANNING YOUR JOURNEY

A journey of a thousand miles begins with a single step.
—*Lao-Tzu*

T he phone rang, and I answered.

David was on the other line. He wanted to know how much a translation would cost. In the world of translation, cost estimates can be tricky. It always depends on the goal and what clients are trying to accomplish.

David told me some competitors told him the cost would be 15 cents per word, but when I asked him what the quote included and if they understood what he was trying to accomplish, he realized the translation and cost might not be that simple.

I talked him through the various factors that could affect the price. By the end of the call, he had a much better understanding of the questions to ask and how to procure a translation. Though David was still learning about the cost of good translations, he knew what kind of problems you can run into by making a poor choice or assuming that the cost is set.

Finding the right translation services company or individual, knowing what questions to ask, and how to get the right translation for your needs takes a little education. A good first place to start is by studying Common-Sense Advisory's research on localization capabilities.

LOCALIZATION MATURITY MODEL

CommonSense Advisory is a research and consulting company that specializes in the language services field. Their research covers pricing, quality, technology, companies in the industry, and more. I particularly like the Localization Maturity Model (LMM) (www.gala-global.org/publications/localization-maturity-model-0) because it shows the developmental stages that a company goes through from the inception of the firm's translation initiatives to becoming a truly global organization that values languages and cultures.

When a client like David calls, we want to understand where on that model his company falls. With that knowledge, we can customize what they need to support their multilingual communications and then advise them on how to improve upon what they are doing.

David's company is in Level 1. David does not have a process, budget, or plan for procuring translation. It is reactionary and price focused.

The following graphic shows the progressive stages in the model.

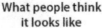

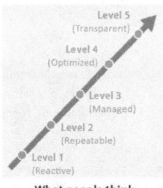
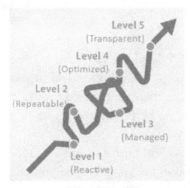

David knows he needs translation for his content, but he thinks he has no way to check the quality and might not understand that translators need training to be successful. With the model, we can give him a vision of how to plan for and procure translation.

First, we start by identifying where he is on the model and then set a vision for where he wants to be. Some organizations might be fine at Level 1. Their needs are not that comprehensive, although they do need translation.

For example, we work with schools that need to communicate with parents who do not speak English. If a school has a large population of non-English-speaking parents, they need to develop consistent and effective ways to communicate. On the other hand, if a school has a limited number of non-English-speaking students, the school does not need as much in the way of translation services. (When they need to send a letter, for example, they can simply translate it.) Notice, however, that this example is not marketing related. Marketing professionals are better served if they are further along the maturity scale.

No matter where you are on the scale, recognize your position and develop a vision of where you want to be.

One of my favorite examples of an organization moving along the LMM is Rotary International. Rotary is a global organization "where neighbors, friends, and problem-solvers share ideas, join leaders, and take action to create lasting change." About 10 years ago, they realized that they had an image problem. People knew of Rotary but did not know what its members did. Many survey respondents thought of Rotary as a secret organization. The culture encouraged the mentality of doing good work without bragging about it.

Rotary's corporate marketing department created US English-based materials and then sent them to the translation department, which had a mixed and reactive process for translating materials. The result: sometimes the translations worked, but sometimes the materials and messages were not culturally appropriate.

The leaders of the translation department slowly turned the communications department into a global communications department.

To do this, they had to:

- Set a vision of being a global communications department.

- Elevate the translation department to be a global communications department reporting into the chief communications executive.

- Implement technology to manage language content.

- Train employees and volunteers on global English writing.

- Integrate a language and culture specialist in the development of new campaigns and content.

- Test the materials in all the priority languages.

- Define who could develop and translate materials by language and country.

- Create brand and messaging standards available around the world.

With a lot of vision and hard work, Rotary is now a leader in global communications.

> To read about their journey, visit
> www.rapporttranslations.com/blog/Rotary-Translation.

The first CommonSense Advisory LMM showed linear progression through each stage of the model. After studying more companies, the organization released the model with the indirect path to show that the journey does zig-zag. Remember, as you begin your journey, it will take focus and time to get to where you want to be.

At Rapport International, we work with clients to progress along the LMM. To support this journey, we develop a Translation Management Plan to define specific actions a client needs to take to reach their goals. Next, I will review that plan to help you further understand how to become proficient at global inbound marketing.

TRANSLATION MANAGEMENT PLAN

Key components to a successful Translation Management Plan

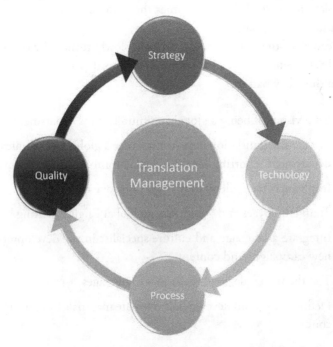

The four key components to a successful Translation Management Plan are strategy, technology, process, and quality. The idea is to continually monitor the cycle and make continuous improvement in efficiency, effectiveness, and cost savings—all of which lead to greater success in multilingual communications.

STRATEGY

First make sure you have a clear company strategy and a marketing strategy and plan that supports your overall strategy. For a template or examples of a marketing plan, check out the HubSpot blog (blog.hubspot.com/marketing/marketing-plan-examples). Your plan expands upon your company strategy and how marketing will reach the growth goals. With a clear definition on what you want to achieve, you have a roadmap for markets and activities to support global inbound marketing.

When your marketing plan defines where you are going, you have a guideline to build your multilingual marketing goals, which will guide you in your decision-making about translation.

TECHNOLOGY

Next, consider the technology needed to meet these strategic objectives. Is your objective to find a fast and easy way to translate reviews on your busy website, or do you want a company to plug into your company portal and seamlessly provide every department with translation? Here are some of the questions to consider:

Is machine translation high enough quality? When AI, machine translation, and Google translate technologies first entered the market, we wondered if they would reduce our business. Instead of decreasing translation needs, we saw these technologies increase the need. Free translation programs work great for getting the gist of a translation and for content clients did not consider translating before—reviews, Facebook posts, junk email, or casual communications. In the past, this content would not have been translated. Now that there is a fast and easy way to translate, people want more translation. Thus, the increasing need for more quality translation of marketing content, websites, and any other material that affects the bottom line or reflects a company's image.

How extensive are your translation needs? If you have small needs, such as a translated web page within your website (otherwise known as a landing page) to describe your services for a test market, then emailing or sharing a document will do. If you have a robust website with continually changing content, you might need a technology connection to simplify the transfer of information.

Is your written material (copy) all new or do you repeat segments? Tripadvisor writers create descriptions in a formula that machine translation recognizes, thus saving time and money. If you have content that is similar (like "dates of travel," "cruise operator," "departs/arrives," "ports"), you might want to build translation memory to prepopulate the fields so only the details need to be entered. On the other hand, if you are a consumer products company releasing new toys, the descriptions will always be new. It is harder to automate fresh content.

Is your copy easily accessible? If you have strict version control and content management systems, it is easier to share the information with the translator for an updated translation. When you track changes, it is easy for the translator to update your materials, whereas if you create and edit content directly on your website, the translator has to read all the content on your site to find changes. Rather than the translator spending the time reading every web page, you can leverage technology to alert your agency or translator to any changes. Then the translator spends time making the changes rather than looking for them.

Will you be doing enough translation to warrant an online platform for translation management? When translation needs get high enough, companies might decide to manage translations through a portal. Internally managed platforms enable you to send translation requests directly to your internal or preferred vendors, or if you decide to outsource, you can find vendors that offer an online platform for translation management.

PROCESS

Once you understand your technology needs, you can begin work on your process. You will need to:

Appoint a person responsible for managing the process. Some clients have an appointed person to manage the translations as one part of their position's responsibilities. Some allow all product managers to request translation, while others have a procurement department. There is no one way to do it. One mistake I see in company processes is that uncoordinated requests lead to lots of minimum charge jobs.

Determine who will do the translations. This decision is a very important factor. In fact, it is so important that I dedicate Chapter 11 to the subject. In that chapter, I discuss benefits and risks of different translation options.

Clarify what will be translated. Again, a good topic that gets a whole chapter. In Chapter 10, I discuss different models to guide you on what to translate. Using one of the models or a hybrid gives you clarity on how to answer whether a document needs translation.

Establish a quality control process. I would be remiss if I did not dedicate a chapter to this subject. You will learn more about quality control in Chapter 9 since many people believe that if they do not know the language, they cannot manage quality. After reading this chapter, you will understand ways to manage quality even if you are monolingual.

Set up a translation request and delivery process. Employees need to know how to request a translation and how much time to allow for completion. A quality translation takes the same amount of time to complete as writing an original document. Allow enough time for quality work.

Establish translation needs and priorities. Refer to your marketing plan. It will help you answer these questions. Plus, reading about what to translate in Chapter 10 will help in those decisions.

Develop document management, version control, and accessibility for leveraging already translated materials. Define those systems early in the process stage to save you time and effort. We have one client for whom we manage their content. We have worked with them for over 30 years, and since their project managers have not been in those positions that long, they come to us for the original English content on products that they want to re-release. We are happy to provide the content for them to edit and then update the prior translations.

QUALITY

It is worth taking time to think about the different levels of quality.

Check out our website for our eBook on Translation Goofs:
www.rapporttranslations.com/content/tidbits-language-trivia.

Just Wrong:
It will give you a laugh but think of the well-respected and financially successful companies that make such mistakes. While people laugh at the errors in translation, it is not very funny for those involved in the campaigns.

Here are some examples:

- "Electrolux—It Sucks." British vacuum cleaner with an advertisement that did not work in the US.

- When Mercedes-Benz wanted to expand into China, they tried using the brand name "Bensi." They quickly learned that they were not selling many cars because "Bensi" translates as "rush to die." Not a great name for inspiring sales!

- When Coca-Cola expanded into China, they failed to realize that their brand name translation meant "bite the wax tadpole" in many areas. And in some areas, it translated into "female horse stuffed with wax." Neither translation inspires one to want to drink the beverage.

- Pepsi Cola did not expand into China unscathed either. When they had their US tagline "Pepsi Brings You Back to Life" translated, the Chinese version actually read "Pepsi Brings Your Ancestors Back from the Grave." I do not think Pepsi intended on starting any zombie rumors, do you?

- When Clairol launched their curling iron called the Mist Stick in Germany, they must have forgotten to do their research. Mist is the slang word for manure in German. Not many women wanted to use a manure stick on their hair.

- When Puffs started marketing their tissues in Germany, they, too, were taken down by German slang. In German, "puff" is slang for "brothel." I do not know about you, but I do not think I would want to use a tissue named "brothel" to blow my nose.

Gist: This is a little better than a "just wrong" translation as you get the idea of what the message is, yet it is clunky to read and might have incorrect grammar. For example, my coworker, Lisa, went on Facebook and read a post that meant to say "Dessert, Pavlova and Crème Brûlée." Instead, it said, "Dessert, Pavlova and Burnt Cream." I sure as heck would rather have the Crème Brûlée instead of Burnt Cream!

Crowdsourced: Some translation agencies offer human translation for cheap prices and fast turnaround. I could not figure out how they could offer their services…until I found out they were crowdsourcing the projects. Cheap and fast is great, yet the risk could be huge. You do not know who does your translation, the translator does not build knowledge of your content and organization, and you lose ownership and confidentiality since your information is all over the web.

Passable: A distributor, internal employee, friend, or family member could do your translation, yet they might not be trained or experienced. They might take shortcuts or change the meaning of your content. Or you could luck out and get a great translation, but the process is not repeatable since that person is not available to translate at times when you need them. With no formal quality control process, this area can be risky.

Solid Translation: With a formally trained and experienced translator, you are more likely to get a solid translation. A good translator is like a good writer. If you like that person's style, you will get thoughtful, enjoyable, and dependable content. Adding a translation editor after the translator completes the first draft gives you assurance that your message is clear. With no editor, there is a chance that a message mistake can happen.

- For example, we translated a tagline for a medical clinic and had a question about the meaning. The tagline said, "It's all about getting better." In English, it has a double meaning: The patient getting better, or the clinic providing better services. The translator read it as the first meaning. The editor read it as the second meaning. Both were right, but in the Haitian Creole translation, the sentence needed a subject. The professional translators knew to ask us to check with the client to see how they wanted to handle this. If only a translator worked on this material, the issue might not have been noticed. The clinic would have had a good and correct translation, yet not understood the nuances.

Sometimes, it is appropriate to have a good translation that can be used in all the countries where the language is spoken. For example, a technical manual for machinery to be used in Spain, Mexico, Argentina, and Chile could be a globalized translation. For these situations, it is best to have a translator, editor, and then an in-country employee review the translation. It would be the same as a good English translation that is used in the US, UK, Australia, and Hong Kong. You can imagine it: the wording might be a little off, yet as an English speaker you would understand it.

Now, let us talk about high-end translations—particularly marketers who want to connect with shoppers. If you live in the US and visit a website to buy pants (or trousers as they say in the UK) and the prices are in pounds, the pictures are of Big Ben and the London Bridge, and they are talking about famous British actors you do not know, likely, you will click away from the site quickly. Consumers are fickle, they want to know that you understand them and can provide exactly what they want. This type of marketing even happens within in the US. I live near Boston; if I buy a baseball glove, I want to see advertisements for that brand featuring the Red Sox logo, the Red Sox players, and pictures of Fenway Park. I am not going to be drawn to one of those other teams! Yes, this product association takes a lot more thought, document management, and attention by the person doing your translation, yet it is the best way to optimize the return on your marketing dollars and efforts.

Once you establish criteria and guidance for your Translation Management Plan, challenges and questions may arise. If suddenly you start getting business inquiries in French, consider the four steps. Is it part of your strategy, and if not, how will you handle the inquiry? If you decide to move forward, are your processes, technologies, and quality requirements able to handle additional translation requests to meet the corporate goals?

As we move through the book, you will understand more about the deeper considerations of each part of the Translation Management Plan.

ACTION STEPS:

1. Identify where you are on the Localization Maturity Model.

2. Set a vision on where you want to be.

3. Begin the outline of your Translation Management Plan to add notes and comments as you continue through the book.

4. Bookmark the page on our website for future reference on developing a Translation Management Page: www.rapporttranslations. com/pillar_page/translation-management-planning.

CHAPTER 6

ATTRACT, ENGAGE, AND DELIGHT IN ANY LANGUAGE

"Pretend that every single person you meet has a sign around his or her neck that says, 'Make me feel important.' Not only will you succeed in sales, you will succeed in life."
—*Mary Kay Ash, Mary Kay Cosmetics*

hat do the following situations have in common?

- Figuring out on the first date whether the person is marriage material
- Negotiating a Chinese business deal over the phone
- Cold calling

Any guesses?

In all three scenarios, no one took the time to build a solid relationship first.

When I started my career in sales, I worked for a company that provided doctors as expert witnesses in workers' compensation cases. My job was to visit attorneys and ask them to send their clients to us for a medical evaluation and a "permanent and stationary" (P&S) report that could be used in court. My job was to sell, but I knew that if I pushed too hard or became annoying, people would not want to see me or send business to my company. I spent time building relationships, so much so that many of my clients became friends.

In those days, I knew the receptionists and many employees in our client's companies. These days, things are different. With current technology, people now search online for information and then only want to talk to a sales rep when they are much further along in the process. Thus, more parts of the sales process are automated.

So, how do you attract and build a relationship online with people who do not speak your language? In this chapter, we are going to talk about building relationships across cultures and language to **attract**, **engage**, and **delight** your audiences.

HubSpot is a company based in Boston that launched the inbound marketing movement. They are a fast-growing and leading provider of marketing platform and sales automation. Rather than a sales funnel where companies find prospects, get leads, and close deals, HubSpot uses a fly-wheel to demonstrate how momentum builds in selling.

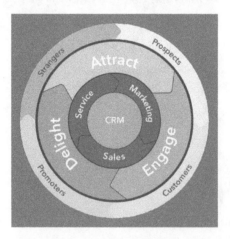

When you employ the HubSpot flywheel, you use the momentum of happy customers to drive referrals and repeat sales. Theoretically, the flywheel is strong at storing and releasing energy. The amount of energy stored depends on how fast the wheel spins, the amount of friction, and its size. Read on as I explain how this model and the concepts of spin and friction relate to global inbound marketing. To read more on the flywheel visit: www.hubspot.com/flywheel.

The flywheel focuses attention on relationship-building rather than on the sales funnel that some sales teams use. The funnel assumes that you need to continually add new prospects into the funnel to earn new business. Whereas the flywheel posits that if you build relationships with your community, new customers will come to you as the flywheel spins without friction.

Amazon gives us a perfect example of an efficiently spinning flywheel. From your first visit to your ongoing relationship, Amazon makes it easy. For the *attract* phase, the products on Amazon come up first in search engines and take you directly to what you are looking for. For *engage*, Amazon quickly gives you reviews and product information and allows you to use one-click ordering. Then, I feel *delight* when I see my fast delivery times and my order records that allow me to quickly reorder.

A huge point of friction arises when your prospects, customers, and promoters do not speak your language. Not providing communications in a person's native language either repels business or at least adds time in attracting, engaging, and delighting—slowing the spin of the flywheel.

MULTILINGUAL COMMUNICATIONS FLYWHEEL

To remove the friction across languages, we used the HubSpot flywheel concept and developed the Multilingual Communications Flywheel.

If your goal is to have clear multilingual communications, then you need to have a Translation Management Plan to communicate with your audiences in the formats that they want. As your communications become more effective and efficient, the faster the multilingual communications flywheel turns, and the more you attract, engage, and delight in the relationships that will grow your business.

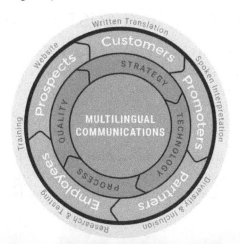

A TRANSLATION MANAGEMENT PLAN HELPS YOU ORGANIZE YOUR BUSINESS ELEMENTS AND BUILD THE MOMENTUM ON YOUR MULTILINGUAL FLYWHEEL.

Now, consider the rings in the Multilingual Communications Flywheel to figure out how to get it spinning. Here are several steps to contemplate:

1. **How:** The first inner ring is your plan. In the last chapter, we talked about the Translation Management Plan. Understanding your company's strategy and goals will define what you want to communicate and how you will do so. Since we spent time on that area in the last chapter, you can refer to it for more details.

2. **Who:** Once you understand your goals, think about your audience. Your first instinct might be to translate your marketing materials and hope to pull in leads. Marketing materials are great to attract visitors, but you also need to think about how you will engage customers. By providing translated training materials, onboarding instructions, FAQs, and company information, you engage customers at the beginning. To truly delight, make sure you provide necessary translation and interpretation along the whole buyer and client journey. Remember to include customer service, return policies, appreciation, and rewards information. Not everything needs to be in-language, just the communications that your customers want.

3. **What:** Understanding your audience will give insight to which communication vehicles you need to translate.

ATTRACTING CUSTOMERS

Looking at a few company websites that do well in attracting multilingual visitors, we can see *how* they meet their goals, *who* they attract, and *what* they translate.

AIRBNB

Airbnb (www.airbnb.com), the vacation rental site, lists rentals around the world. The listings offer anything from a room in a house to a full castle. With an international presence, the site needs multilingual accessibility that makes it easy to use in any language. They have done a good job in building a platform that accommodates all users by incorporating the following:

- Standardized platform: Consistent labels and patterns for entering basic information like number of guests, bedrooms, and bathrooms means readers can access information in any language.

- Images: The ability to upload multiple pictures eliminates the need for long descriptions.

- Amenities: A standard checklist of amenities shows whether they are included or not.

- Sleeping arrangements: Shown with graphics rather than words.

- Standard calendar: Recognized by all users.

- Standard map: Recognized by all users.

- Rules: A checklist of images appears on the property page.

- Internet Protocol (IP): Programmed to pick up the user's preferred language for using the platform.

Only two open response areas need to be filled in. By standardizing as much information as possible and giving multiple choices for the options, Airbnb keeps it easy for owners to enter details about a property and for renters to check out properties, no matter the languages they speak. Talk about *engaging* and *delighting* in this part of the process!

The property and location descriptions are the two open response areas in language. Airbnb handles this aspect with an easily accessible Google Translate option. Here is an example from my own experience. For years, I have wanted to visit St. Petersburg, Russia. So, I searched places in Russia and found an apartment owned by Alexander. The standard description met my needs, but I could not read the Russian description. Lucky for me, right beneath the Russian text was the option to translate. I saw the Russian description and the translation.

ORIGINAL CONTENT:

"Квартира расположена в самом центре города. Короткая пешая прогулка, и вы уже на Невском проспекте. В этом районе вы откроете для себя основные достопримечательности города: Эрмитаж, Дворцовую площадь, Летний сад, Исаакиевский собор и многие другие."

GOOGLE TRANSLATION:

"The apartment is located in the city center. A short walk and you are already on Nevsky Prospekt. In this area you will discover the main attractions of the city: the Hermitage, Palace Square, the Summer Garden, St. Isaac's Cathedral, and many others."

The Airbnb disclaimer reads: *This description was automatically translated from Russian using Google Translate and may not be completely accurate.*

As you can see, the English is translated with grammar errors, but you get the meaning or the gist of what it says. This quality is standard for Google Translate, yet rental owners accept it because they want to attract visitors from all over the world and they are not going to pay to formally translate their descriptions into 10, 20, or 30 languages. By offering an easy Google Translate link, Airbnb opened the world for their customers. The translation quality is good enough for me to want to stay there, as I can read about the nearby attractions. Airbnb has figured out a way to make language translation cheap, fast, and accessible. Machine translation works for Airbnb as it delights customers with the ability to get the gist from the quickly translated descriptions in any language. We will delve deeper into when to use Google Translate and when to avoid it in Chapter 7.

Now, reviews are a different consideration. The reviews are in English, Russian, Spanish, French, Chinese, German, Japanese, Korean, Swedish, and more. There is no way to translate the reviews automatically. Yet, it shows me that people from all over the world stayed there. (Plus, I can read the Spanish and French reviews well enough to know they were positive.) A number ranking system also shows me that out of over 100 reviews, Alexander got 4.99 out of 5 stars on the property. It is clear enough without reading all the reviews that the apartment is a nice place.

Alexander's challenge may be in communicating additional information to renters: Check-in time, access, parking, kitchen, time-zone adjustments, special rules, etc. If he thinks through the typical questions he gets from renters, he can develop and translate one correspondence to answer the questions in the most frequently used languages. The information must be clear and concise for a good translation and if other random questions arise, he can pop them into Google Translate to get the "gist" of the meaning. At that point he can decide how to reply, either with a high-quality translation or a Google Translate reply.

NIKE

Another company that sells effectively to global consumers is Nike, which focuses on delivering innovative products, experiences, and services to inspire athletes. Products include sports clothes, sneakers, winter jackets, swim goggles, balls, and more. Athletes, as they say, are "anyone who has a body."[37]

Nike's marketing strives to elicit emotions from customers because that type of connection encourages consumers to buy their brand. The company does not have customers posting on their site and it has very well-developed marketing messages. The site needs to have high-quality content and images.

Nike's site (www.nike.com) makes finding your home country easy with the navigation at the top right. Instead of a drop-down button to display languages, you choose your country. Sorting by country allows the user to see culturally preferred products in their region.

For example, even though both the Mexico and Argentina sites are in Spanish, the products for Mexico customers are the same ones featured in the US page, which is in English. The duplication tells me that buyer preferences for products and activities are more similar in the US and Mexico than in Argentina (assuming Nike closely researches buyer preferences, which I believe they do). You also see that even though the sites for the US, Indonesia, Malaysia, and the Philippines are in English, the products and the images for the US site differ greatly from the sites of the other countries.

For example, consider one of the running shoes I like: The Nike Air Pegasus, my preferred running shoe for over 20 years. The original English copy is short, snappy, and clearly written.

Breathability and inspiration come together in the Nike Air Zoom Pegasus 36 Premium Rise. A knit-in graphic repeating across the mesh and synthetic upper spells out, "Just Do It" in perforations. Strategically placed, they cover zones where your foot releases the most heat.

- *Shown: Crimson Tint/Luminous Green/Orange Trance/Black*

The Spanish copy on the Mexican site, professionally translated, clearly describes the product.

La transpirabilidad y la inspiración se unen en el Nike Air Zoom Pegasus 36 Premium Rise. El gráfico incorporado en el tejido que se repite a lo largo de la parte superior de malla y material sintético está hecho con perforaciones que dicen "Just Do It." Estas perforaciones están colocadas estratégicamente para cubrir las zonas donde el pie libera más calor.

- *Color que se muestra: Tinte carmesí/Verde Luminoso/Naranja Trance/ Negro*

If I put the Spanish translation into Google Translate, the meaning is not as short or snappy. The English sentence has 17 words and reads clearly. The translated copy has 27 words and is clunky. Plus, I'd rather have "luminous green shoes" than "light green shoes." One sounds so much fancier and faster!

Breathability and inspiration come together in the Nike Air Zoom Pegasus 36 Premium Rise. The graphic incorporated in the fabric that is repeated along the upper part of mesh and synthetic material is made with perforations that say "Just Do It." These perforations are strategically placed to cover the areas where the foot releases more heat.

- *Color Shown: Crimson Dye/Light Green/Orange Trance/Black*

If I go to the Uruguayan site and search for this shoe, I do not find it. The website or country managers watch product purchases and know what will sell in the different markets. They know their buyers and put information on the site to bring in locals.

By the way, on the US page, the price is $73.90; on the Mexico page, the price is MX$2078. For a moment, I had a shock, until I remembered that Nike was also smart to localize prices on each country site. (FYI, $74 equates to about MX$1500, so the shoes are less expensive in the US.) I bring this up because if you customize your website to sell internationally, remember after you pick the right products, translate your content, and add culturally appropriate images, you need to list the prices in the correct currency. If Nike organized their website by language instead of country, currency conversion would present a challenge for them.

Airbnb and Nike are examples of two consumer-facing companies that show how to effectively use translation on a website. Nike localizes their content to make it particular to each country.

Business-to-business services and product manufacturers have more flexibility in globalizing their content translation. For example, Conitex Sonoco (www.conitex.com) offers *packaging that doesn't slow you down.* The business sells and has offices in countries all over the world. We translated their website into three other languages: Spanish, Indonesian Bahasa, and Simplified Chinese.

Company management chose one Spanish translation even though they have offices in Spain and in Mexico and sell in other Spanish-speaking countries. Having one translation works for the company because buyers must work with sales representatives to get exactly what they need. The sale is complex and needs human involvement for guidance and delivery. To attract and connect with people online, doing a single Spanish translation to connect with potential buyers works.

In addition, Conitex Sonoco sells different products in each market, so the content translated into Spanish was not the same as the content translated into Bahasa and Chinese. Management focused their translation efforts on just the content appropriate for the country and language.

To read the case study about Conitex Sonoco visit: www.rapporttransla-tions.com/case_studies/conitex-sonoco-translate-website.

As you can see, your multilingual marketing strategy varies depending on your company and overall marketing strategy. After you figure out how to attract visitors to your website, you need to engage them. Again, your industry, company, and goals will differ in the way that you do this. Fortunately, there are ways for you to do it with only English-speaking employees.

ENGAGING AND DELIGHTING ACROSS MULTIPLE LANGUAGES

Airbnb might be able to avoid using multilingual service representatives if the platform is built so well that users never have any questions. Imagine anticipating the questions that customers have and answering them all on-line. Conversely, a manufacturing company that consults with customers on highly technical materials or processes probably needs to have employ-ees or distributors who speak the language.

There are many ways to handle multilingual communications. Look at the following 4 x 4 matrix, which shows the options for handling different levels of volume and engagement needed to best serve your customers.

MULTILINGUAL ENGAGEMENT OPTIONS

Engagement		Volume	
		Low	High
	High	Telephone interpreting Video remote interpreting (VRI)	Bilingual employers In-country distributors Live chat
	Low	Chatbots Website	Web content Blogs Resource center FAQs Videos with subtitles

Engaging is the process of figuring out the best way to communicate. Delighting is using your tools to anticipate and react to what customers want.

Engagement: High engagement means that the sale is complex, and your customers need sales and service involvement to get their needs met. Low involvement means that customers have quick questions and will be happy with online answers.

Volume: High volume means that you have a lot of inquiries in a specific language, like Spanish. Low volume means you have few inquiries in another language, like Mandingo.

Once you understand the particulars on the scale, you have the following options to engage with leads and customers. Here is more information about the services available to connect with a person who does not speak your language:

HIGH ENGAGEMENT/LOW VOLUME

Telephone Interpreting offers a quick, on-demand way to handle over 200 languages without hiring many bilingual people. Your customer service representatives can conference in the customer and within 20 seconds have an interpreter on the line to facilitate the conversations.

Video Remote Interpreting (VRI) increases engagement by connecting people through video. Since most communication is done with body language, having a video call with an interpreter on the line brings more understanding and engagement.

LOW ENGAGEMENT/LOW VOLUME

Chatbots offer an easy way to anticipate questions, translate the copy, and feed the answers automatically when asked in a specific language. A little planning goes far in automating answers in target languages.

LOW ENGAGEMENT/HIGH VOLUME

Website Copy can attract and engage leads and customers during the buyer's journey. If you answer the "big five" questions (see Marcus Sheridan's book, *They Ask You Answer,* for more information) in the target languages, you show that you care about your customers, no matter their language.

Resource Centers take your website even further by offering a way to sort by topic and format of the content. For example, when you post translated blogs, videos, white papers, and guides to your website, customers can go there for answers rather than contacting you. Just remember to add subtitles or voice-overs to the videos to make them accessible in other languages.

HIGH VOLUME/HIGH ENGAGEMENT

Bilingual Employees work best for high-touch, high-engagement industries. If you decide to hire bilingual employees, implement programs to attract, engage, and delight them, or you will have a revolving door and frustrated managers. In a later chapter, I talk about best practices for building a culture that celebrates inclusion and bilingual employees.

In-Country Distributors can be your link to customers that do not speak English. Even though the distributors might not speak perfect English, they might communicate well enough to facilitate industry specific business. Government resources and global trade groups can help you find an appropriate distributor.

Live Chat is best for customers who have questions and want quick answers over the chat function on your website. With high-engagement customers, you can hire and train bilingual employees to answer questions in either language or make sure chat connections go to representatives that speak the desired language. If you do not have enough requests or access to bilingual staff, you can outsource your Live Chat services just as you would your call center.

> To listen to a webinar about conversational marketing through live chat, visit www.rapporttranslations.com/blog/conversational-market-ing-in-a-global-online-world-free-webinar-august-2nd-2018.

GLOBAL RELATIONSHIPS

As you can see, you can handle multilingual communications in many ways to **attract**, **engage**, and **delight** customers. Moreover, what you need in one language might be different for other languages. The bottom line is that you need to remember that you are forming relationships. Consider what you need in each quadrant and each culture as they differ in expectations of business relationships.

With high-engagement and high-volume relationships, keep in mind cultural differences. Researching the countries you plan to do business in by doing a quick search online, asking your language service agency for advice, or talking to people from the country can give you tremendous knowledge. Most Americans get to the point. They figure, why waste time with small talk? In many other countries or even different parts of the US, however, you do not do business with someone whom you do not know. In China, for example, it would be highly unusual to negotiate a deal without an in-person meeting. Such meetings include group meals with specific seating arrangements and conversation about non-business topics. In Mexico, you would talk about families. In Japan, it is common to give appropriate gifts. Understanding how to build culturally appropriate relationships is important in global marketing.

For low-engagement and low-volume relationships, fast and easily accessible information is what the customer wants. By meeting that need, you are forming a relationship appropriate for that interaction.

We spent this chapter looking at relationships, expectations, and connecting with other people. Since technology is developing and changing fast, we need to look at technology and how machine translation, AI, and other advancements are confusing or simplifying multilingual communications.

ACTION STEPS:

1. Discuss with your team how your organization performs across the attracting, delighting, and engaging flywheel.

2. Look for ways to improve your success by using the flywheel model.

3. Outline how you can adapt your flywheel activities in another language.

4. Determine where your content falls in the Engage/Volume grid.

CHAPTER 7

MACHINE VERSUS HUMANS

"I fear the day that technology will surpass our human interaction.
The world will have a generation of idiots."
—Albert Einstein

W hen I bought a translation company in 2004, people asked, "Who needs translation?" A few years later, people gently inquired, "Is Google Translate going to put you out of business?" Now people ask, "Can you provide quality translation that is culturally appropriate?" People get it now: not all translation is the same.

Google Translate launched in 2006 as a statistical translation program (machine translation), then 10 years later, Google released a neural machine translation (NMT) or artificial intelligence translation. I interchange those terms in this book. Regardless, understanding the differences and viability of these technologies is important.

Machine translation translates one word at a time. In simplified terms, it recognizes a word and spits back the translation. It works well for simple words like dog, hello, or chair. Artificial intelligence looks at phrases and sentences and predicts the translation. That process works well for simple and direct content like "what's the weather today?" or "may I have a drink?"

Both technologies opened the world to other languages. Suddenly, people could type in their language and "talk" to someone else. Machine translation offered lots of memes and jokes with some of the translations produced. Yet, we used it.

Artificial intelligence advanced the quality by looking at phrases or sentences and predicting what the person wanted to say. Programmers called it "deep learning," and we thought it meant that the machine offered deep thinking. Really it meant that more levels of programming are in the technology. The deeper levels saved storage memory in the programs, produced "better" translations as increased program usage influenced predictions, and enabled the technology to go directly from one language to another without English being the common language.

Sounds great right? Just put the artificial intelligence Google Translate plug-in on your website and you will be set. Here is a very simplified example to show how those methods work.

Do you know the TV game show *Wheel of Fortune*? It is like the game "Hangman." Basically, the player guesses a letter to fill in the blanks to make a word. In our scenario, the word is a sentence, and each letter represents a word. Machine translation gives the meaning of each letter, and it can only go one letter at a time. Artificial intelligence guesses each letter but also looks at the word, trying to fill in the blanks. It does not understand the meaning.

In contrast, trained human translators understand the meaning, emotion, and cultural differences of the word while also filling in the blanks of the whole sentence or paragraph. If you have a simple sentence to translate or one that you use repeatedly, machine translation or artificial intelligence could work. But if you have content with a specific meaning, there is a good chance that some or all the meaning will be lost in the translation.

At times and in certain situations, artificial intelligence translation serves a useful purpose in business. Given the focus of this book, I am purposefully leaving out the uses for individual consumer use in travel, interpersonal relationships, and other low risk uses of free and easy translation.

(A great article on machine translation is avaiable at www.theatlantic.com/technology/archive/2018/01/the-shallowness-of-google-translate/551570/.)

LIMITATIONS OF AI: CASE STUDY 1

Ken Kahn, the owner of Oh! Toys called us for translation in an interesting situation. Sales of his building-block marble-run toy started skyrocketing on his website, and he wanted to know why. He followed the electronic trail back to a Japanese website that gave a highly positive review of the specialty marble run.

Since he does not speak or read Japanese, he called me to ask for a translation of the website to find out what they were saying. When we quoted the price for the whole website at $2,000, we both knew that translating the whole site to get the information he wanted did not make sense.

I suggested that he look for the part on the website that referred to his product and run it through Google Translate. Our company philosophy is to help the client in the best possible and least costly way. In referring him to the free translation software, we did not lose $2,000. We gave good advice and gained a loyal client.

He soon came back to us because when he ran the content through Google Translate, it said that his toys stimulated the "ass part of the brain." After a little chuckle, Ken decided to send that part of the website content to us for translation so he could really understand what it said. It was a $200 project, and the accurate translation said the "3D block puzzles stimulate an area of the brain called the precuneus, which is responsible for understanding spatial structures." That explanation was great messaging that he could use on his English-language website.

Ken's Oh! Toys translation is a perfect example of how to leverage machine translation to determine what you need to translate.

> You can read the case study on the Rapport International website: www.rapporttranslations.com/case_studies/oh-toys-case-study.

EFFECTIVE USE OF AI: CASE STUDY 2

Tripadvisor is the world's largest travel platform that allows users to browse, review, and book accommodations, restaurants, events, airlines, and cruises. The service is available in 49 markets and 28 languages. To be able to offer the information in 28 languages, Tripadvisor has strict English writing requirements and a set pattern for internal writers. By following those requirements, the artificial intelligence program can translate their website content quickly. Tripadvisor knows that by teaching the humans to adhere to the processes of artificial intelligence, the company can leverage the technology appropriately. Since Tripadvisor is a fast-moving technology company that developed training for employees, the following requirements work well for them.

- Be clear.
- Write in short sentences.

- Avoid the use of humor, slang, and colloquialisms.

- Write in an active not passive voice.

- Follow a prescribed pattern.

- Use standard words.

In visiting the Tripadvisor site, you can see that the descriptions of places follow a format. The consistency makes it easy for readers because they know what to expect, and the format is easy for artificial intelligence since the patterns are the same.

Tripadvisor has done well with leveraging artificial intelligence for its website platform. (On a side note, the company still has translators on staff to handle more complex communications for the legal department, social media advertising, and partner communications.)

INTERPRETING ISSUES: CASE STUDY 3

Picture the United Nations' meeting room. People from all over the world listen to a speaker who may not speak their language. Everyone has access to a headset that broadcasts their language of choice. The highly qualified, simultaneous interpreters sit in booths in the back and work 15-minute shifts to relay the message of the speaker. Multiple booths accommodate all the languages. That arrangement is high-end interpreting for important global discussions. It is high-cost, high human involvement, and takes technicians to manage. You see this option at high level conferences.

Now, imagine conferences happening all over the world with people who want to listen in their native language, yet do not have the option. Instead of listeners struggling to catch the complete meaning, new artificial intelligence technologies translate the presentation in a live feed on an app on each person's phone. It is amazing technology that offers clarity to attendees who would not have had access to any supporting interpretation.

Like Google Translate, NMT is not culturally adapted or completely accurate yet, but it gives access to those who would otherwise have nothing to assist in understanding. It is a more affordable option for conference planners who want to make their content more accessible to all. It is extremely impressive.

As you can see, with a thoughtful and strategic approach, companies have success with artificial intelligence. With a strategy, process, and the right technology, artificial intelligence can lead to productive communications, particularly in situations where no language accessibility would exist otherwise.

However…for companies that use artificial intelligence as a low-cost alternative and hope to get the same results as a high-end application, we see many risky and worthless uses of the technology.

POTENTIAL PROBLEMS

Before jumping in to using Google Translate or NMT, we ask you to consider these potential problems:

1. **The translation is not accurate.** We took a simple statement *"Cut the clutter with paperless billing"* and translated it into Simplified Chinese. Then we used Google Translate to back-translate it into English. The result was, *"Use paperless bills to reduce confusion."* Google Translate captures a gist, but it sounds stilted, unclear, and the meaning has changed.

2. **You spent time on your marketing message, and Google Translate does not capture the meaning**. Here is an example from Mazda. The company's tagline in Japanese is *Jinba ittai*, which captures the feeling of a Japanese mounted archer. Essentially it means "Imagine. You are one with the horse as you soar across the land ready to shoot your bow and arrow. It is that moment of perfection in the feeling of movement." A few months ago, when we first put Jinba ittai in Google Translate, it translated the phrase as "danger." If you try it now, it translates as simply "jinba," or sometimes it says, "one horse." Either way, the meaning is wrong, and it lacks the feeling of the original phrase. Can you imagine Mazda using the slogan *"Drive a Mazda—it's your one-horse car!"*

3. **Languages do not work.** If the program is not installed correctly and then tested, the selections will not work. That problem makes the company look sloppy and not committed to the non–English-speaking market. We have seen websites with plug-ins that do not work. Make sure to test everything on your website.

4. **It only partially works**. On some sites, the text in the body of the page is translated, but the headers, footers, and call-to-action buttons are not translated, or vice versa. Try reading a site that is half translated—for an example check out www.Cpsenergy.com and click on "Español." The headers, footers, and some text appear in

Spanish, but the main content and all the graphics remain in English. The missing translation will frustrate your Spanish speaking visitors who will immediately leave your site.

5. **Increases your risk.** We have seen currency exchange companies, law firms, and other regulated-industry companies risk liability by using Google Translate. Businesses that require precise language need to avoid machine translation. Making a wrong claim or giving false or confusing information because Google Translate just gave a gist translation puts the company at risk.

6. **It is not culturally appropriate.** Google Translate translates the words, but what about the colors and pictures as well as the cultural references? In some countries, the pictures of people must reflect their stature. Higher ranked people or respected older people must sit taller in the picture. In the US, we would never notice the position of an individual in a marketing picture, but it is important in some Asian countries. Remember the *Wheel of Fortune / Hangman* game example? Google Translate can get the word but not the meaning.

7. **Does not reach your audience**. The company 4Tests (www.4tests. com) offers free practice standardized tests. One of the tests is the Test of English as a Foreign Language (TOEFL) exam, which is the test that foreign students are required to take to be accepted to a university in the US. The website offers great advice about preparation. For example, they advise not to learn English solely from movies and TV but to study content that students would see in a college course. Even though users may speak English well enough to comprehend the instructions, they may want to read it in their native language to make sure they can pass the test. Or maybe their parents, who will be paying for the test, may not have strong English skills and need the information. Instead of providing good, clear translation on the information, 4Tests.com buried the Google Translate plug in at the bottom of their website. The company is undoubtedly losing money by not accurately translating their advice and making it accessible to potential clients.

8. **Does not engage the customer.** When you go to a website, you want to see that the company understands what you need and can meet those needs. Google Translate does *not* sound like a native speaker. You lose your readers if you do not take the time to give them easily accessible, culturally adapted information in their na-

tive language. In today's world, we are surrounded by content. If it is not engaging and easy to consume, people move on quickly.

9. **The language picker is difficult to find**. Many website developers think they are offering a good translation option, yet it is a wasted effort if the language picker is in the footer. Having it buried at the bottom of the page makes it difficult to find even if the website is in your native language. Imagine someone who speaks a different language trying to find it at the bottom of a page they cannot read! Check out www.oregon.gov or www.nationalgrid.com and scroll to the very bottom to see an example. Maybe they meet the government requirement for accessibility but it is not user-friendly.

10. **The languages in the picker are in English.** If a non-English speaker even finds the Google Translate drop-down menu, is it in their language? Typically, the languages are in the language of the website. Imagine that you are on a Chinese website looking for the language picker to switch it to English. Your first problem would be finding the language picker. Then, you have to know how to find "English" in the Chinese characters. That dilemma alone makes the plug-in practically useless to put on your website.

Advances in artificial intelligence are exciting and fun to watch. The technology offers connections across languages that we dreamed of with "mind melds" or the vision of the Polish linguist L. L. Zamenhof in creating one language: *Esperanto*. Instead, technology offers a clickable button to immediately get the gist of what someone says.

Language is ambiguous, flexible, and fluid, so we see areas that will unfortunately never adapt to machine or AI translation. We consider Google Translate (NMT) as the "gateway drug." People see it as the free and easy way to translate their website, but once they realize the inherent quality issues, they ask us, "Do you make translations that are appropriate for the audience and their culture?" When we help them think through their Translation Management Plan, we look for ways to leverage the technology in appropriate ways.

In the next chapter, we will look at other ways that technology is changing the delivery of language services.

ACTION STEPS:

1. Check out your website to see if it has the Google Translate plug-in installed.

2. Delete the Google Translate plug-in if it is there.

3. Start a glossary of consistently used words or content that can be translated once for multiple uses.

4. Imagine a case study about your multilingual communications. Would it be an embarrassment or showcasing good work?

CHAPTER 8

SUPPORTING TECHNOLOGIES

"Energy rightly applied and directed will accomplish anything."
—Nellie Bly, journalist, and record-breaking trip
around the world in 72 days

When I bought Rapport International in 2004, there were tremendous opportunities to add technology into the business. The prior owner, Lisa Gavigan, started the business in 1987 before companies had websites and databases. Standard processes included paper mock-ups of layouts, FedEx mailings, and index-card rolodexes. She had the capability and interest in the technology changes yet had lost passion about the industry. I lucked out. She was ready to move on, and I was excited about how technology could enhance Rapport International.

Fast-forward to today and, as in all industries, technology permeates all that we do. In the last chapter, we discussed technologies used by people to do translation and interpretation. Now, I want to talk about how technology changed the way the industry operates.

This chapter gives you an overview of how technology assists in the processes. Since your processes and your service provider may use these technologies, I will introduce you to them, so you have an overview of the options and what to expect.

PROJECT MANAGEMENT: PROCESSES, PLATFORMS, AND PORTALS

Written translation can range from home-grown internal platforms to client-facing portals. The value of the platform is to manage the flow of the translation.

Process: Shown below are the steps that written translation projects go through during the management process.

- Intake
- File prep
- Questions to client
- Assign translator
- Respond to any translator questions
- Diary due date from translator
- Receive project from translator
- Send to editor if needed
- Track project
- Send edits to original translator
- Reconcile any differences
- Clarify any meaning with client
- Finalize with translator
- Get client approval
- Edits to translator to review
- Finalize with client
- Quality review
- Send to layout if needed
- Get client approval
- Finalize layout and send to printer or upload to website

Companies vary in how they go through this process, but they ultimately reach the same goal of a high-quality translation. For example, on most projects that we do for our client TOMY, the designers send us a word document for translation. Most of the time, they do not request an editor, internal reviewer, layout, or any specialized services since they have internal reviewers and designers who work on the layout files themselves. They just need the translated content to drop into the final layout. Their custom process includes the steps they need. For each project or client, we adjust the process to meet their objective.

Platform: A platform is an environment for building and running applications, systems, and processes. Platforms can be viewed as toolsets for developing and operating customized and tailored services. The platform is the internal technology that a company uses to manage their processes.

For example, one internal platform that we have enables a client to save time by notifying us of their blog updates. They publish a blog to their website every month and rather than them sending us a document in MS Word and us returning the translated version to them to upload, we built an alert into the website to tell us when a new blog publishes. The alert notifies our platform to pull the English language content so it can be sent to the translator. When it is done, we can electronically push it back up onto the website. That ability saves the client steps in their process as well as the time needed to publish the translation. In such situations, the platform or toolset for facilitating the processes exists internally at Rapport International.

In another example, we have a client that has their own proprietary platform for employees to request translation. The client wants to send a notification to us to log into their system and download the projects. That interface allows them to track the projects internally. In this case, we have a portal to their internal platform.

Portal: A portal is a website or web page allowing access to a password-protected site—in other words, a doorway. A portal allows clients to upload, determine the status, and download completed translations through a login to access the language services agency's website. Some of our competitors developed portals for clients to use. The agency drives the process that clients must follow. The agency does not adapt to their clients' processes.

A few years ago, we considered building a portal for our clients. Ultimately, we decided not to build a translation portal after talking to our clients, because they told us they did not want another website to log in to and administer. They preferred having us fit into their preferred processes. If a client has an internal platform and wants us to work within that application, we connect through their portal to provide language services. Even though it is not as efficient for us because we must adapt to each clients' technology and process, we stand by our values of what makes us different:

figuring out the best way for the client to get what they want.

Again, it is your strategy and preferred process that drives your use of technology. A portal, whether it is internal or provided by your agency, only offers an advantage if it fits into your process.

Since we work with a variety of clients at Rapport International, we built a system to accommodate our clients. We chose to develop an **internal client-management platform** (with no portal) for translation yet offer a **client portal platform** for spoken interpretation. Below, I explain the differences in more detail to deepen your understanding.

RAPPORT EXAMPLE 1: INTERNAL CLIENT-MANAGEMENT PLATFORM

For written translation, many busy clients find translation to be yet one more challenge when getting work done. They want an easy hand-off, fast turnaround, and assurance that it will be done right. They do not want to learn and use another technology. We spend time understanding what "easy," "fast," and "good" means to them and then set up a process to meet their needs. If we did not have a 100 percent on-time delivery record, clients might want a portal to show them exactly where in the process their projects stand.

RAPPORT EXAMPLE 2: CLIENT PORTAL PLATFORM

While translation clients want varied ways to send us written projects, people who schedule in-person interpreters want easy and fast ways to schedule. Some schedulers want to call, others want to email, and some want to schedule online. In this case, we offer a scheduling platform through a client portal with secure access for people who want to schedule online and offer telephone, email, and fax options for others. Interpreter schedulers are a different buyer with immediate needs, and we found that offering a portal simplified the process for those who wanted it.

From those examples, you can see that language service providers offer options to fit the needs of the clients they serve. As you begin your search for the right vendor, keep in mind what works best for your specific needs.

OTHER TECHNOLOGY ADVANCEMENTS

In addition to project/assignment platforms, there are industry specific technological advancements. They are:

Translation Memory: Translation memory (TM) is a key technological development in the industry. TM is a specialized translation tool that does not do the translation but helps professional translators stay consistent when working with a client on an ongoing basis. TM software takes the source file to be translated and segments it into smaller portions. It then compares those segments to already translated files and automatically fills in a suggested translation, which allows for more efficient translation and consistency of voice. Even when a translator or agency uses TM, a professional translator reviews the full translation for quality and completeness.

Think about the "About Us" section used on your website, annual reports, brochures, presentations, and more. Companies that consistently use the same description benefit from being clear in describing who they are and what they do. With TM, your repeat copy stays consistent across each translation.

Remote Interpreting: This gives you the ability to connect with an interpreter on the phone or over video in under 30 seconds. To access these services, you set up an account, dial a designated number, and speak to an operator who then connects you to an interpreter in almost any language. These services are also known as "telephone interpreting," "over the phone interpreting (OPI)," "video remote interpreting (VRI)," or "Zoom interpreting."

When the world shut down due to the COVID-19 virus and conferences and meetings went virtual, conference interpreting platforms quickly adapted to accommodate simultaneous interpreting across multiple languages to meet these needs.

APIs: API stands for application programming interface, which is a software intermediary that allows two applications to talk to each other. Previously, I talked about Lisa, the prior owner of Rapport International, having to FedEx original and translated content back and forth to clients. APIs allow us to connect to websites and pull the content to our translation management platform. Rather than mailing or emailing content, through technology we can pull it to our platform, translate it, and then push it back onto the client's website.

The interface works great for websites, proprietary software platforms, Google Docs, and more. It saves time in sending content back and forth and eliminates risks of forgotten or dropped content. For larger and technical content, an API is a very handy tool.

Foreign Language Layout or Desktop Publishing (DTP): Files done in Quark, Illustrator, Publisher, or other design programs need a specialist to replace the English content with the translated content. Typically, designers are not used to working with foreign fonts, spacing, line breaks, texts, and design elements in the files. Designers design; foreign language DTP specialists understand the intricacies of laying out other languages. Technologies evolved over time to allow for the right-to-left reading requirements of some languages and for global fonts.

To read more about DTP, visit www.rapporttranslations.com/blog/ foreign-language-desktop-publishing-explained.

Remote Interpreter Training: Although we only hire trained and experienced interpreters who we test and qualify, some companies offer virtual training for interpreters. The need for interpreters continues to grow and the availability of trained interpreters cannot keep up. Interpreter training consists of one or two semester-long classes, a degree program, or a community class. The limited availability of these classes contributes to the shortage of access to trained interpreters. Online training has opened more flexibility for those interested in pursuing a career in interpretation.

As with all industries, the language services industry leverages technology to advance accessibility of services. When I bought Rapport International over 15 years ago, I launched a website and transferred contacts from index cards to a Customer Relationship Management (CRM) system. Now, our VP of Operations manages multiple platforms to simplify access for clients and to streamline internal activities. It is exciting to see what the next 15 years will bring.

ACTION STEPS:

1. Visualize how your company would look with global marketing as part of the process.

2. Document any current processes that you have now for translation work.

3. Assess the gap between your vision and your current processes.

4. Repeat this exercise for technology (no need to list what the technology is, just what you want it to do).

CHAPTER 9

FIVE STEPS TO HIGH QUALITY

"Good communication is just as stimulating
as black coffee, and just as hard to sleep after."
—Anne Morrow Lindbergh, American author, and aviator

A huge change in awareness about translation quality comes from four merging dynamics: Google Translate, worldwide access to the internet, millennials' experience with global travel, and increased buying power across the globe. Seasoned marketers now understand how important a quality translation is for marketing materials.

Think of the last time that you selected a new doctor. Of course, you knew you wanted a good one. Why was it hard to find one? Not understanding medical qualifications or having insider access to information makes it difficult and leads to concerns like, "Will I get quality care?" and "Is this the right specialist for me right now?"

This chapter discusses the need for high-quality translation rather than an automated or quick translation. Later, in Chapter 12, we will look at some of the funny results of lower-quality translation so that you can assess the risks of not building quality into your translation process. The following five key points demonstrate the best way to get the quality you need.

1. **Take care of your responsibilities.** With your heath, you know that if you eat right, drink water, sleep well, exercise, and get an

annual physical, you have a better chance of staying healthy. The same is true for translation. Here is what you can do to get your translation processes healthy.

a.   **Provide well-written documents.** The saying "garbage in, garbage out," also applies to translation. If you eat garbage, your doctor will have a hard time keeping you healthy, right? Likewise, if you provide content with grammar mistakes, unclear messages, typos, and/or incorrect spelling, the translator will have a hard time converting your text into a high-quality translation.

b.   **Write in "Global English."** Your message is all about being clear. If your doctor spoke in medical jargon, would you get the message? For translation, if your content includes slang, colloquialisms, sports references, incomplete sentences, and silly word play, the meaning will likely be lost on your audience. In the US, people use baseball references frequently. They say, "Let's hit a home run this year." In other countries, those words mean nothing to people because they do not play baseball. By writing in clean, clear English, you are more likely to have people engage and understand.

To learn more about writing in Global English, visit www.rapporttranslations.com/blog/good-translation-starts-with-good-writing-global-english.

c.   **Develop a process.** Even without realizing it, you have a process for seeing the doctor. You go for an annual check-up, call the nurse for quick medical questions, or schedule an appointment for any lingering sickness. When you go for an appointment, you check in, give the nurse a history first, and then talk to the doctor. Just as you have a process for taking care of your health, you must have one for translation. Decide what will be translated, determine who will manage the process, who is involved in the quality control, and determine the translator/agency expectations. Set timelines and expectations, just as you do with your doctor when she says, "Take this and see me in a week if you do not feel better."

d. **Communicate clearly.** If you only tell your doctor that you are "sick," they have little information to help. Your doctor must ask you further questions. It is the same with your translator. Good language services partners want to know what you are trying to accomplish, who your audience is, and answers to any questions that arise. By being accessible and providing responses to the questions, you will get a higher quality translation.

e. **Provide final content for translation.** Version control across languages can be very difficult and costly. Providing the final copy at the start saves time, liability, and costs. Plus, a good translator aims to keep a consistent message and "voice" for the document. Submitting finalized content makes that work easier.

Remember the formula: Quality in = Quality out; Garbage in = Garbage out.

Even the most careful content providers occasionally let mistakes slip through. Untrained or sloppy translators might dismiss typos, incorrect dates, inappropriate cultural references, and poorly written text. Check with your provider and ask if their translators and project managers communicate these finds back to you. You want to work with a partner that wants your best work to shine.

2. **Find the right specialist.** Even if you are diligent about taking care of your health, sometimes you need a specialized medical professional. A few years back, I broke my leg while skiing. After a visit to the Emergency Room for an x-ray, the ER doctor recommended that I see an orthopedist, which is a specialist in broken bones. He did not suggest an optometrist or proctologist because they were not the appropriate specialists for my needs. Again, the comparison is the same with translation. Here are some of the different options you have.

a. **Bilingual employees.** Many companies and schools opt for internal employees because it seems like an inexpensive and easy option. Yet, managers often do not consider the "lost opportunity costs" of having employees do the translations. Opportunity cost is the lost value of what the person could have been doing instead of translation. The doctor's office may save money by having the x-ray tech take *and* read the x-ray, but the tech is trained to take it and the doctor is trained to read it. By substituting an unskilled employee for a professional translator, you take your employee away from the job she is trained for and risk not getting the quality you need.

At Rapport International, we hear anecdotes about bilingual engineers being asked to translate marketing material. Would you ever ask your engineer to write marketing material? Translating is like writing; you get better quality with the right person on the job.

b. **Distributors.** Exporters often rely on in-country distributors to translate materials. Again, this option can be an "inexpensive" option and save time. Yet, is it the best choice? Medical device representatives have deep knowledge about their devices and teach the doctor how to use it, but it is the doctor who has greater knowledge of how to care for the patient. The doctor leans on the representative for advice but does not let the representative do the job. By letting your distributor do the translation, you lose control of the message being sent to the market. You are the doctor in this scenario; you have greater knowledge about the global corporate marketing message that you want to send. Unfortunately, your message can be lost in translation by distributors who speak English well enough to converse with you but may not have a deep understanding of the nuances of the language. Or they may choose to change your message to one that is more sales-based rather than marketing-based. Marketing talks benefits, sales talk features.

Plus, if you operate in more than one country that speaks the same language, using in-country distributors for translation might result in different translations in the same language (for example, you sell in Mexico, Argentina, and Spain and each distributor provides a translation and website content). That option actually ends up costing more and increasing liability for you. Have your distributor do what they do best: sell. Later, when you decide to consolidate your website and have a single translation, you will be thankful that you retained translation and message control from the start.

For a good discussion on this topic, listen to *The Global Marketing Show* podcast interview with Randi Roger at www.theglobalmarketingshow. com/e/english-not-the-global-language/.

c. **Any bilingual person.** Prior to breaking my leg, I had a pain in my shoulder and could not get it to go away with stretching, rest, or physical therapy. My primary care doctor recommended a visit to an orthopedist practice that scheduled me with Dr. Re. After a shot of cortisone, I was better. Since I had good success with him, I called to schedule with him for my broken leg, but they scheduled me with another doctor, a leg specialist (who did a great job fixing me). The point is, just like orthopedists who are specialists in particular repairs, even if a person is fully bilingual it does not mean she can provide a good translation. A good translator also has the following:

   i. **Experience, training, or certification.** While anyone can apply a Band-Aid to a minor cut, it takes a specialist to stitch a deep cut. Likewise, many people can speak two languages, but it takes a specialist to provide a high-quality translation. A good translator is an excellent writer, knows proper grammar in both languages, asks for clarification if the meaning is not clear, references dictionaries for accuracy, and does research to capture the meaning. When a professional translator reads a word that has no equivalent in the other language, they know how to convert it. Not just anyone can write your content, just as not any bilingual person can translate your content.

   ii. **Right language.** In addition to having the above qualifications, good translators are native speakers of the target language. The source language is the original, and the target is the needed translation. A good translator is equally proficient in both languages yet only translates *into* her native tongue, which ensures that the message is correct and culturally appropriate.

   iii. **Right location.** Determine if the translation needed is region-specific. Linguistic nuances and cultural differences can arise frequently, especially in marketing copy. Expressions and idioms are also very region-specific, so know where your material is going and try to find a linguist who is familiar with that specific area's customs as well as language. In the Boston area, for example, we use the saying "wicked smart" to describe someone who is very intelligent. In the South, you frequently hear people say "y'all" when they address even one person. But I never hear "y'all are wicked smart." The two regional sayings just do not go together.

iv. **Subject matter expertise.** Is it marketing material or general communications? Each type takes a different set of skills. At Rapport International, we assign a different translator to marketing materials than we assign for an electrical engineering patent application. Make sure your translator has subject matter expertise.

d. **Machine translation.** I devoted a whole chapter (Chapter 7) to this topic. The bottom line is that if you want quality in your translations (or from your doctor), do not use a machine.

e. **Independent translator.** If you can find an independent professional translator with whom to build a relationship, that arrangement can work well. The price could be lower than working with a professional agency but you take on more responsibility. You manage the process, quality control, deadlines, glossaries, document management, and if the translator becomes unavailable, the responsibility is on you to find another. In the right situation, it might be fine, as long as you recognize the risk.

3. **Build your team.** Physicians rarely work alone; they have staff such as receptionists, nurse practitioners, physical therapists, nurses, physician assistants, and others who support them. Good translators often work for agencies because they offer similar support: a scheduler, project manager, editor, quality control, account representative, and layout specialist. The translator focuses on her specialty, and the agency supports her work and communicates

with the clients. Plus, a good agency gives best-practice suggestions and helps the clients reach their goals.

4. **Develop your support team.** When you are diagnosed with a serious condition, you may want a second opinion, and once you make your decision, you want a team you can trust. If you ask your doctor for a recommendation for another specialist to give you a second opinion, a good one will give you the name of another respected professional. Your doctor is your primary trusted advisor, and you rely on her for guidance. Think of your translation project manager the same way: if you want a quality check or have questions, work with your project manager. The more information you share, the better your team will get at providing the services you want. As mentioned earlier, we work with one company that asks us for original copy on products they want to re-release. They know that we keep their original documents and translations in order. The advantages of building a team include:

   a. **Matchmaking.** When you see the same doctor for your annual physical, she gets to know you. With linguistic matchmaking, the same translator works on your content so that over time, you develop a consistent voice, and the translator gains deeper knowledge of your material and company.

   > Read more about linguistic matchmaking at
   > www.rapporttranslations.com/blog/linguistic-matchmaking.

   b. **Internal reviews.** If you have internal employees, distributors, or partners that want to review the material, you can build that step into the process. With a consistent team, everyone understands what will happen at each stage.

   c. **Terminology.** Just as you build a relationship with your primary care doctor over time, you do the same with your translator. They learn your word choices, styles, and preferences.

   d. **Communication.** Typically, your initial doctor visit or translation project takes longer. As your relationship builds, you become more efficient in communicating as both of you come to understand expectations and responsibilities.

5. **Focus on quality**. Using our medical example again, a doctor's focus is not solely on quality control; it is also on continuous improvement. If your staff's primary role is only looking for mistakes, they will find them. Conversely, if the focus is on continuous education, process improvements, and better communication, the results will improve *and* naturally you will find and fix mistakes in the process. Here are some suggestions on this aspect as it relates to translation:

   a.   **Establish goals.** Understand the goals for the project or the year. If the team understands why you are doing the translation, everyone can watch for ways to improve.

   b.   **Leverage technologies.** In the same way that your doctor's office upgrades technology by offering online portals for access to information, virtual appointments, insurance submissions, testing capabilities, and website links for sharing information, watch for ways that you can leverage new technologies to improve access to language services. Over our years in business, we added an online scheduling portal, document transfer capabilities, translation memory, quality measurements, client satisfaction surveys, a language services education library, video training, conference interpreting automation, and more. Keep in touch with your agency to learn the ways that they can help you.

See more at www.rapporttranslations.com/learning-center

   c.   **Open communication.** The longer the team works together, the better communication typically gets. Keep an ear open for ways to improve. Make sure feedback loops are open and that everyone is satisfied with the quantity and quality of information they receive. Is the information timely? The only time we miss deadlines is when we have to wait for clients to answer our questions. Getting good quality translation is a team effort, just as staying healthy takes a partnership with your health providers.

   d.   **Test when appropriate.** Certain translations need market testing, just as certain medical conditions need tests to move forward. If you create taglines, brand names, or search terms, test them. Years ago, we translated a packaging description for a successful US product called Take & Toss— inexpensive plastic containers that you could reuse or dispose. American consumers liked having the option to keep or throw them away. The products flopped in Europe because consumers there wanted clarity on whether the product was reusable or disposable. The company created a new name for specific European countries, "Säva." We tested the name across six European languages and the product subsequently launched successfully and still sells in those regions.

To read the case study about Take & Toss, visit www.rapporttranslations.com/case_studies/tomy-international.

Just as it takes effort to stay healthy, it takes effort to get a good-quality translation. Clients looking for a quick fix or who focus only on remedying problems will struggle more with communicating clearly across languages.

Here are two ways people try to check quality that I recommend avoiding:

Pitting providers against each other. This attempt entails hiring a second agency and asking them to check the first agency's quality. This is *not* a good strategy. Any doctor can find an issue with how another doctor treats. You are better off asking your current agency to have an editor review the translation. Two great minds working together bring better results.

Translating back into the original language. Otherwise known as back translation, this involves having a second translator convert the translation into the original language without seeing the source document. It is a waste of time and money. If you have a good translator and editor, they will create a translation with your message intact. A back translation is not going to be exact, just as if you gave two people a writing assignment to describe an evening meal. Many words are different and mean the same thing; in the US, the terms dinner and supper are interchangeable. If the translators use interchangeable words, the translation will differ from the original. Again, it would be like asking two people to write content about the same subject and then comparing them for quality. Everyone's style is different. Plus, a back-translation costs as much and takes as much time as the original translation. Usually, we are only asked by life sciences companies to provide back translations for documentation for the FDA. Otherwise, get a good translator and editor team, and get a certified translation by an independent agency with liability insurance, experience, references, and a quality guarantee.

The point, as for any project, is to build your team with experts in each role and then focus on continuous improvement.

ACTION STEPS:

1. List out the materials that you want to translate for each stage of the buyer's journey.

2. Identify what materials need high-quality translation.

3. List out the possible resources for translation.

4. Consider whether your chosen translation resources can give you the quality you need.

CHAPTER 10

WHAT: FRAMEWORKS FOR DECIDING WHAT TO TRANSLATE

*"There is no way anything of value can be done without some framework.
It might well be that the framework is discarded, or the rules opposed;
that is not important. What is essential is that they exist so that
one knows when one is in opposition to them."*
—*Dame Margot Fonteyn, British ballerina*

E arlier, in Chapter 5, I introduced you to the Translation Management Plan, which is a starting point to develop a strategy. Part of creating a strategy is figuring out what you need to translate to meet your goals. Although it may seem like an easy question to answer, with a well-thought-out plan, you will save time and resources by clearly defining which documents need to be translated.

There are a few ways to decide what materials need translation before people start asking for translations. Of course, you can always be responsive to requests, but with a construct for deciding what to translate, you can plan and budget to meet your goals.

Here are some frameworks to consider:

DEFINE THE CONTENT FOR TRANSLATION IN YOUR MARKETING PLAN

A good marketing professional creates or updates a marketing plan each year to set goals for the coming year. Typically, the goals focus on brand recognition and revenue growth. One goal could be to enter new markets; if that market is in another country, include related translation goals, even if you expect to have clients who are bilingual.

Even if your prospects speak English and that is the language you conduct business in, a little added translation effort can go a long way. A few years ago, we did translation for a client who was presenting in South Korea to a group of executives who spoke English. Our client learned that their firm won the deal because they translated their PowerPoint presentation into Korean, even though the attendees spoke English in the meeting. Little gestures have big meanings in cross-lingual communications!

When entering the global arena, US companies typically start with other English-speaking markets, such as the UK, Canada, Australia, or New Zealand. From a language perspective, this approach make sense, but a better method is to determine which countries have the best market for your products or services. Why compete with all the other companies entering English language markets if you can sell more by providing translation for a bigger return? Best practices recommend doing a market analysis to figure out the markets with the best return.

Listen to *The Global Marketing Show* podcast with Nina Ann Walter of Expandise to learn more about how to research new markets: www.theglobalmarketingshow.com/e/steps-to-global-ecommerce.

For example, if you sell a product in the UK, where five other competitors also sell it, but in France, there is only one other competitor and the total market demand is the same as in the UK, by spending a bit on market research and providing French translation, you can substantially increase your revenues.

Unfortunately, many leaders miss big opportunities by being afraid of "other" languages. A trade advisor once told me that language was the number one fear of exporters from the US. By learning ways to handle language communication successfully, you can grow in markets around the world.

If you already have new clients contacting you from other countries, that is great! Instead of having to research market opportunities, you already have a starting point. Figure out why those customers buy from you and make sure that reason aligns with your current marketing message. Use this information to develop a framework to guide you as you expand into new markets.

There are a couple ways to do this. You can start with one product/service and increase offerings over time in a region, or you can take that one offering and expand to other geographic areas. By tracking and measuring successes and interests, you can measure demand and work to increase interest in your company.

EASY ANSWERS TO THE BIG FIVE QUESTIONS

Recently, I got a call from a potential client, Joseph Gray from DRMetrix, a company that monitors advertising across more than 130 national television networks in the US. Internationally, DRMetrix helps companies in the electronic retailing industry by tracking the amount spent on TV advertising by US companies for retail products. As there is a correlation between media spend and product success, companies investing in these TV products for international markets look to DRMetrix's data to guide their product investment decisions. He wanted to translate emails he was getting from foreign companies asking about his services. Then he wanted to have his responses translated. The back-and-forth process would take multiple independent translation projects. After talking to him about his request, I suggested instead that he answer the big five questions on a landing page and point visitors to that page for answers to these questions.

Typically, the questions are about:

1. Cost and pricing.
2. Problems the customer is trying to solve.
3. Comparisons to other solutions.
4. Reviews or feedback on your services.
5. Best-in-class comparison to competitors.

If you would like more detailed information about this topic, check out Sheridan's book, *They Ask You Answer*.

In Joseph's situation, he can do one translation to answer anticipated questions from the buyer. Ultimately, he saves money as translating the landing page costs the same as translating a couple of emails. The additional answers provided on the landing page gives the added benefit of bringing the client much further along on the buyer's journey (more below). Plus, offering the information on the website in popular international languages allows many more potential customers to see answers to the same questions.

By taking the time to think through what he was trying to accomplish, he saved time and money in reaching multiple international markets.

BUYER'S JOURNEY

If you are in marketing or sales, you may be familiar with the buyer's journey framework, which outlines the process your client goes through before purchasing a product. The journey begins when buyers realize that they have a problem. To solve the problem, the buyer searches for solutions and eventually decides how to solve the problem. Marketers classify the stages of the journey as attract, engage, and delight. During all the stages, the buyer is looking at different types of information.

For example, let's look at the Chinese customer at DRMetrix. The buyer is a manufacturer of consumer products who wants detailed information on products selling successfully across all modalities—internet, TV advertisements, and more. This information drives decisions on what they manufacture.

The Inbound PR Methodology

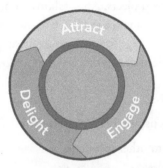

Attract Tools	Engage Tools	Delight Tools
Content	Email	Email
Blogging	Newsroom	Social media
Press releases	Live chat	Events
SEO	Bots	Exclusives
Social media	Meetings	Feedback
Video	Calling	Inbound links
Ads	Social media	Analytics
Knowledge base	Marketing automation	Marketing automation

www.hubspot.com/inbound-marketing

Attract: Also called "awareness," at this stage you want to provide information that will make the buyer *aware* of your company and then proceed to visit your website. The buyer realizes that they need more information to understand what products or services might solve their problems. They would like to have a greater understanding about the different options available. They start to research what might be out there to solve their problem. They will start looking for:

- Blog articles
- Guides and white papers
- Industry reports

Engage: Once the buyer finds a solution to their problem, they start engaging with companies that offer possible solutions. In our example, the buyer reached out to Joseph at DRMetrix in this stage because preliminary research showed that DRMetrix had the solution to their problem. As buyers consider solutions, they want more detailed information about working with a company, such as:

- More in-depth blogs
- Comparison white papers or e-books
- Webinars and podcasts
- Product feature videos
- Live chat and sales calls
- Pricing and product details
- Demonstrations or consultations

Delight: An often-forgotten stage of the journey is *delighting* the buyer in the final stages of the sale and post-sale engagement. Once a prospect becomes a client, continuing engagement works to build a long-term relationship. Clients value further education and communication. Information such as:

- Progress reports and updates
- Service delivery improvements
- New product/service offerings
- Best practices

As a marketing expert, you spend time developing content to attract clients. When considering the different stages of the buyer's journey, are you providing information in each stage to "speak" to your non-English-speaking prospects?

BUSIEST PAGES

Another way for marketers to decide what to translate is to look at website traffic. Which of your web pages do people visit most and stay on the longest? Metrics on traffic provide insight into what content your prospective customers value.

A Maine-based consumer products company came to us for translation after their marketing agency noticed that a few product pages were getting visitors from Korea, yet they did not stay long. By adding a landing page in Korean that talked about the company, the products of interest, and how to order, the company saw their orders increase. Watching their website traffic helped them identify a new market.

For service companies, maybe your blog drives a lot of traffic to your site and people navigate to other pages from there. Start by translating the blog and optimizing it for the search engines; pay particular attention to keywords and search phrases. (In Chapter 13, we will look at special consideration on search engine optimization (SEO) and keyword translation.) Once you translate the blog, consider your buyer's journey. Assuming that they are in the "attract" stage when they find your blog, decide on information that you can provide to move them through "engage" to "delight."

TEST AND TRACK

If your products sell online and you want to test new markets, you can create translated landing pages, optimize those pages, and track the results.

Cleverhood, a company that sells beautifully crafted rain ponchos that are stylish and functional (particularly if you bike in the rain), called us because the company got a STEP grant to translate their website (see the Resources section at the end of the book to learn about getting grants for translation).

Cleverhood knew that Japanese consumers bought their ponchos in a few stores in Japan. With the STEP grant, the company wanted to increase awareness about its products in Japan, both their availability in stores and how to buy directly online. Although the website offers many beautiful products in addition to their ponchos, the grant did not cover translation for the whole site, so the company chose certain products to highlight online. By having specific pages translated, Cleverhood can track online visitors and interest in specific products and increase translated product offerings as sales increase. Starting with limited products or services is a great way to test and grow a market.

4 X 4 MATRIX

Say you figured out that you want translation but your budget will not support translation for all your products/services. You will need to prioritize what to translate to get the biggest return. Creating a 4 x 4 matrix is one way to narrow down your options.

Earlier, I mentioned a client, TOMY, and I will refer to their practices for this example.

TOMY is a leading global designer, producer, and marketer of a broad range of innovative, high-quality toys that kids and parents love. Brands include *Lamaze, John Deere, The First Years, Boon, Thomas the Tank Engine, and more.*

Typically, parents buy the toys at stores, so eye-catching packages that attract them to the product are important. Then, with good translations of the user instructions, parents can set up and use the products with their children. Even though TOMY has delightful English web pages, videos, focus groups, and more, the company chooses high-quality translation for its packaging and user information at buying opportunities. TOMY knows easily accessible and accurate translation is important for sales in the US and abroad.

High

Packaging User manuals Product information	Website for online ordering
Landing page with product description	Videos Focus groups

RETURN

Low   *High*

COST

By plotting out the costs and returns of your translation investment, you can easily see what materials you might want to translate first.

TOMY understands that packaging, manuals, and user instructions will help buyers travel through the decision stages faster because customers historically make purchases at stores. On the other hand, TOMY needs to invest more into language services if they want to hold multilingual focus groups or adapt to new online ordering behaviors.

In this chapter, we looked at a variety of ways to help you prioritize your translations needs. Whether you respond to buyers' requests, use the big five questions, select materials for the buyer's journey, track your busiest pages, test and track, build a matrix, or a combination of all these options, be thoughtful about what you choose to translate. By using a framework or a hybrid, your team can build a consensus around a budget and priorities as you enter new markets.

After you decide *what* to translate, it is time to figure out *who* will do it. In the next chapter, I discuss how to select your translator. As you read through the chapter, think about what you need translated as you consider who will do your translations most effectively.

ACTION STEPS:

1. Review your content to make sure it answers the big five questions.

2. Decide on content to translate for each stage of the buyer's journey.

3. Listen to this podcast featuring Michelle Safrit to hear her talk about how Conitex Sonoco decided what to translate: www.the-globalmarketingshow.com/e/handle-website-translation/.

CHAPTER 11

WHO: ASSIGNING THE RIGHT PERSON FOR YOUR MATERIAL

"There are two kinds of people: those who do the work and those who take the credit. Try to be in the first group; there is much less competition."
—*Indira Gandhi, Former Prime Minister of India*

After you decide what you want to translate, you must figure out who is going to translate for you. Do you ask a bilingual friend to translate, or do you hire an agency? Are there other viable options? In this chapter, I explain the options and risks associated with each course.

Deciding on a translator is not easy...you do not want to be the person who embarrasses your company or client by getting low-quality or laughable translations.

These are some well-known marketing translation mistakes:

- "Got Milk?" was translated into "¿Tienes Leche?" for Spanish-speakers, which means "are you lactating?"

- Pepsi's slogan in the 1960s was "Come Alive." The Chinese mistranslation enticed people to "bring your ancestors back from the grave."

- "Nova" made headlines as a branding mistake. The story goes that in Spanish, "no va" means "it doesn't go," yet the car name is one word, so it made for a funny translation story. This one is an urban legend because Chevy's Nova actually sold well in Mexico and Venezuela.

Here are some mistakes that smart clients brought to us for review before launching their content:

Community Health Center: The marketing team used a staff member to translate a communications booklet about benefits. The untrained staff member translated the references to "mobility aids" to "AIDS," as in the illness! Luckily, the team asked us to review the translation. Our reviewer became irate about this and other mistakes in the booklet because of the potential liability to the client due to not hiring a professional translator.

Manufacturer: A company decided to have their in-country distributor translate their marketing materials and website into the local language. Unbeknownst to the company, the distributor changed the meaning and messages of the original content. Instead of translating the marketing messages that talked about the benefits of the product and why it was better than the competitors, the distributor changed the message to talk about the features, measurements, and prices. Luckily, they had us review it and point out the differences in the messaging.

User Manual: The head of a marketing firm found an independent French-speaking expert to translate a user manual into French. The company received many complaints from users in Canada about the word choice and quality of the translation. Once our Canadian French translator reviewed the manual, she clarified that the former translator spoke French from Haiti. Although the translation was good for use in Haiti, the nuances of grammar and word choice made it look sloppy in another French-speaking market.

Marketing Slogan: The creative team at Staples developed a fun campaign that included talking about "refrigerator art." In the US, refrigerator art refers to our kids' masterpieces, which we hang on the refrigerator to celebrate their talent. When translating the campaign into French, our translator explained that in France, people do not have the equivalent of refrigerator art. With good advice from the translator, the client knew to skip that part of the campaign in France.

Professional Services Company: The marketing team needed a white paper translated for inbound marketing, so they asked one of their professional consultants to do the translation. On prior projects, the translation was good because the consultant is fully bilingual and understands the material. The team came to us with the translation request because the consultant had commitments to a client and could not complete the translation in a timely manner. Not having a predictable process or a consistent voice for translation caused challenges for the marketing team.

As you can see, by not carefully choosing your translators, you may run into higher costs, even though it seemed cheaper at the outset. Plus, you might run into difficulties or quality issues with your multilingual communications. The key takeaway is to pick the right option for the material that you need translated.

As we look at all the options in choosing a translator, some might seem less or more expensive. It is important to remember the hidden and indirect costs that accompany the choice of not using a professional translator. Indirect costs include:

- Lost revenue from the assigned employee not doing their regular job, particularly if the position is revenue-generating.

- Wasted time by not using a more efficient professional translator.

- Lack of document management or version control for translation.

- Missed deadlines due to time constraints.

- Risks of not using a professional agency with liability insurance.

- Grammar mistakes made.

- Incorrect messaging or meaning due to lack of training and language skills.

- Cultural gaffes.

THE OPTIONS: RISKS AND BENEFITS

The different options for translators include:

- Family/Friend
- Distributor
- Employees
- Crowdsourcing
- Independent Translator
- Language Service Agency/Provider (LSA/LSP)

This chapter covers human translation. Of course, machine translation is also an option, and I dedicated the whole of Chapter 7 to that topic.

FAMILY/FRIEND

Over the years, I have had many calls from prospects who confess that they reached out to family and friends when they needed business content translated. In virtually every instance, they eventually ran into problems and needed to figure out how to have the content professionally translated.

How can you know who to trust with your words? A person you already know well can be a good choice. They know you and your preferences, they are willing to do the work, they may not charge you for it, or they may charge you less than other options.

Watch out for issues. Yes, your friend or family member may be able to speak the other language well, but are they grammar fanatics? Do they completely understand the deeper messages of each language and culture? Always consider how well they know *both* languages.

Also, consider the writing ability of the person. Who among your family or friends is a great writer who can be trusted with your content? In my family, I can think of two great writers, my mother, who is a professor in criminology and writes textbooks, and my son, Robert, who is a sophomore in college majoring in agriculture. Both are fantastic writers but have no marketing knowledge or business writing experience. Always consider the writing skills of the bilingual person you choose.

Benefits: Inexpensive, personal connection
Risks: Quality, liability

INTERNAL EMPLOYEES

A company—let's call them Zeus Corporation—assigned their in-country marketing people to do their translations. The advantages were that employees understood the company and industry lingo, were accessible, spoke both languages, were motivated to do well, and could tell the corporate marketing department when the message did not align with the local culture. They also were available to answer questions at any time.

But the plan did not work as well as expected.

- **Translating the monthly content took a week to complete.** The in-country marketing people spent a week sitting at their desks rather than organizing and attending trade shows and supporting their local sales representatives. Accounting for the salaries and lost opportunity costs of their marketing and selling time, the company spent more money than if they had hired a professional translator.

- **Diluting the global messaging.** The corporate marketing department developed global messaging, but the message got diluted when it was sent to regional offices for translation. Spanish translations were done by different people in Spain, Argentina, Peru, and Mexico so they lacked consistency in writing and terminology. By coordinating translation in the corporate office, the company would have saved money and protected the global message.

- **Risking the quality.** The in-country marketing people spoke English well enough to speak and email with corporate, but they did not have an in-depth understanding of English, nor did they have formal translation experience. Sometimes, messages were lost in translation, and since there was no formal review process, mistakes were not found until much later.

- **Changing the meaning.** There were a couple of times that Zeus' corporate marketing found out that the regional marketing person changed the text's meaning. Each time, the person explained that the message did not seem right for the local market, so they wrote what they thought worked. Corporate spent a long time researching and refining the messages; using a local marketing person for the translation can inadvertently change messaging on an individual whim. In contrast, a professional translator would work with corporate to explain the problems and make recommendations, so that the people in charge can make an educated decision how to handle any translation issue.

- **Cost-benefit analysis.** Ideally, companies pay an employee to do specific valuable work. If an employee makes $75,000, the fully loaded costs for that employee are about $97,000 with benefits, vacation, taxes, and other costs. Let's say a company wants to make a 30 percent gross profit margin on that employee's fully loaded costs. The employee's value to the company now becomes $138,571. If you divide that value by 2,080 hours worked in a year, the result is about $67 per hour. Estimating that a person takes about four hours to translate a 1,000-word document, the lost return on the work that your employee could have otherwise been doing in their specific position is \$268. Using a professional translator would cost about \$250. In addition, as the amount of copy increases, the differential in lost productivity also increases.

Bilingual employees make great in-country marketing people, customer service representatives, sales representatives, managers, and executives, yet without training, they are not usually the best people to do your translation. A better use of bilingual employees is to have them review the translations for company and industry terminology.

Benefits: Know company and industry terminology, availability
Risks: Quality, messaging, lost productivity, hidden costs

DISTRIBUTORS

Your distributors are motivated to get your translations done; they know that content in their local language will help them sell more. Remember the research from Chapter 4? Over 70 percent of bilingual audiences want content in their native language, and more than 56 percent of the people polled will spend more on purchases if the content is translated.

Distributors want to sell and will get your translations done and out to clients quickly. They know the audience and the culture, so it will be culturally adapted. And often they might not even charge you. Sounds like a great deal, right?!

As with any great deal, there are trade-offs. Besides having the same issues as with employees regarding quality and version control, you might have further problems. Here is an example where a company ran into problems with their distributor doing their translations:

A company I will refer to as Bambi Industries searched for and hired a distributor to sell its emission control products in France. Along with the agreement on how the distributor would sell the products, the distributor offered to translate marketing and sales materials. Bambi Industries trusted that the distributor would handle the translation in an efficient and sufficient manner.

Over time, it became clear that there were problems.

- **No visibility in the market for the new client.** The distributor worked with dozens of companies, hence the good reputation in France. A few of their top products sold fantastically well, hence the good feedback when Bambi Industries called for a reference. Yet, as time progressed, Bambi's products did not sell because the distributor's salespeople were focusing on the already successful products.

- **No urgency given to translation.** Along with the lack of attention in sales, the distributor did not translate the materials expediently. Again, they focused attention on providing information on the proven products.

- **Incorrect message conveyed.** When the translations were finally done, the company saw their content mixed with content from other products and companies. They did not provide clear, differentiated messaging on Bambi Industries' products. The company suffered a lack of visibility as a result.

- **Lost website clicks.** Driving people to your website increases the search traffic. The distributor used the company's content on their website without links or references to the company's home site. The company lost control of this when they gave the distributor permission to translate and use the content.

- **Changed messaging.** Bambi Industries hired the distributor to sell and then agreed to have them "write" marketing content, even though they would not have asked their own salespeople to write the marketing content as they knew marketing and sales are two different skills. In the translation, the distributor changed the message to focus on price and features, as many salespeople would, rather than communicating the value, differentiation, and benefits of their products provided in the company's original messages.

- **No access to a clean French translation for future use.** When the company decides to launch in another French-speaking country, they will not have a good French translation to start with, either for their globalized launch or to localize for the new market.

If you do have your distributor do your translation, make sure you have a Translation Management Plan (Chapter 5) to manage your translations.

Benefits: Maybe cheap and fast, one less thing for you to do

Risks: Losing control of messaging, content, inbound marketing; multiple uses of translation

CROWDSOURCING

Earlier this year, I was at a conference and came across a booth for translation services. I noticed their extremely low prices, so I stopped in to check it out. I asked the representative how it was possible to provide human translation (not machine translation) at such a low cost. The answer was *crowdsourcing*.

At first, I thought, "Cool, it is like the Uber of translation."

Then, I shivered and walked away with a gut reaction to the potential for issues. Here are just a few things that came to mind during my conversation with the representative:

No confidentiality. With crowdsourcing, you are posting your content onto the web so that anyone can access it. All confidentiality is lost. If confidentiality is important in your business, crowdsourcing is not a good choice.

Lost ownership of copyrights. Similarly, once your content is online for the crowd to translate, you have lost the ability to call it your own. Any copyright protection that you have is now lost to the cloud and the crowd.

Poor quality translations. We are careful to assign translators who understand a client's material. As they continue working with a client, the translator is gaining knowledge about the company, its materials, products, services, and industry. With crowdsourcing translation, you can have different people working on your material at different times, and you cannot be sure who is overseeing the quality and consistency in a particular language.

No accountability for issues. If you have a crowd doing translations and there is a mistake or the project is late, to whom do you go to address the problem? With linguistic matchmaking, your consistent relationship with the translator means that the designated person can develop ongoing knowledge. You also avoid repeat mistakes or issues due to this relationship. Because you are not selecting the translator when crowdsourcing, there is no one person to train or hold accountable.

Little accessibility for questions. If a question comes up about your translation and it has been done by someone in the crowd, how do you access them to ask about it? Or if the original English is not clear and the translator needs to understand what you are trying to convey, how do they contact you to ask questions? With little or no accessibility, you might not get what you intended.

No liability insurance to protect you. As a professional translation company, we carry liability insurance. If there is ever a grave mistake, we have coverage that helps protect our clients. Thankfully, we have never had to access our liability insurance coverage in over 30 years, but with crowdsourcing, your liability risk is not covered.

No consistency for multiple projects. Say you use crowdsourcing to translate your website. Then, you have a brochure to translate so you go back to crowdsourcing. If the person who translated a product name did it one way for your website and the person working on the brochure translates it differently, it will cause a lot of confusion for your brand....and your customers.

Benefits: Cheap and fast, step up in quality from machine translation

Risks: Loss of confidentiality and ownership, no long-term knowledge built about your company, liability risk

INDEPENDENT TRANSLATOR

With Google and sites like Rev.com and Upwork, you can easily find individuals who work as independent contractors. If you hire and develop a direct relationship with an independent translator, you get the advantage of working directly with that person to develop a workflow and maintain a consistent voice. The translator continually gains deeper knowledge about your content. In good relationships, you develop a comfort level and grow together.

If you work with one language and have limited demands, that arrangement is a reasonable solution.

Clients who have hired independent translators eventually go to agencies for a few reasons.

- **Demand:** One person can only handle so much. Over time, as your translation demands increase, one translator might not be able to keep up. What happens if your translator has an emergency? Maybe you have so much success with one language, you branch off into other languages, then you become the agency as you manage all the translation projects.

- **Logistics:** A good agency will help with document management, best-practice advice, and layout requests. Individual translators focus on translation and not the supplementary services.

- **Quality Control:** When you receive content written in English, you are the final quality control. You can read it and make sure you like it. When you get the translation from an independent translator in a language you do not speak, make sure that you have quality measures in place. Options include a review by an internal bilingual employee or distributor or having a second translator edit the documents.

- **Technology:** As in other fields, technology is changing rapidly in language services. Make sure your translator is keeping up with any technology that you might want to use for your content.

Warning! Even though translators may tout translation certifications and experience, they might not be qualified for your project. Over the years, we have tested multiple, seemingly qualified individuals just to find out that their style is "off" or their translations are awkward. Carefully judge a translator's writing style and consistency, just as you would when hiring a writer for your content.

Benefits: Direct relationship, build knowledge about each other
Risks: No ability to scale, lack of quality control, you have to handle project management

LANGUAGE SERVICE AGENCY/PROVIDER (LSA/LSP)

As you can surmise, hiring an LSA or LSP to translate your content is the full-service option. The biggest negative in the short-term is the price. The biggest challenge is hiring the right agency.

To learn more about hiring the right translation agency, watch this vlog at www.rapporttranslations.com/videos/8-traits-translation-company.

Let us summarize the benefits.
The benefits of working with the *right* agency are:

1. Qualified and trained professionals are doing your translation, so you know it will be correct. A qualified and trained translator needs to have the same skills as a writer *and* be fully bilingual.

2. High-performing translators; the agency gets consistent feedback about its translators from multiple clients and reviewers.

3. Unbiased party who will ask for clarification on any inconsistencies.

4. Intermediary who can facilitate feedback between you and the translator for brutal honesty.

5. Timely translations so that even if an emergency happens, the

agency can juggle competing priorities to meet your needs.

6. Cultural appropriateness feedback to alert you when your content is not appropriate for your audience. The agency project manager and the translator will watch for that aspect of translation.

7. Quality control in real time. The agency will work with you to build appropriate processes to deliver the quality you need.

8. Document management and version control. The ability to provide original content when a company wants to re-release a product, which saves time and money.

9. Confidentiality and ownership. By working with an agency, your work is confidential, and you retain ownership of all content.

10. Ability to handle fluctuations in demand. As you grow and your needs change, you can easily scale up or down to meet needs. Your employees have an immediate resource to get translation work done.

Benefits: High-quality results, process and project management included, best-practices suggestions

Risks: Higher costs, particularly if you hire the wrong agency

HYBRID MODELS

Of course, using just one of the options previously discussed might not suit your needs. Many experienced companies that do substantial amounts of translation develop a hybrid model to determine who will translate. The specific content, quality needs, and availability of resources influence who does the translation. Here are two options of hybrid models for you to consider.

OPTION A: LIABILITY RISK MODEL

One view is that for high-risk materials, you should use an agency, whereas for low-risk materials, you can leverage other resources.

Low Risk ————————————➤ *High Risk*

Unsolicited emails	Revenue/earnings communications
Employee casual chat	Marketing materials
Light competitive research	Legal contracts
Gist translations	Regulatory/authorization forms
Light email communications	Training
	Sales proposals

OPTION B: RETURN ON INVESTMENT (ROI) MODEL

Another way to look at a hybrid model is by cost and return.

High

One-on-one sales communications Revenue/earnings releases	Website Videos
Unsolicited email	Landing pages Social posts

COST (at left, centered vertically)

Low   *High*

RETURN

In using this model, plot your content and then prioritize what you want to translate. From there, you can adapt the cost/return on what you can leverage from already translated materials.

For example, in year one, your sales proposal might be expensive to translate for your first client. Yet, in subsequent years, it is low cost and high return since you can reuse the original translation and just edit the client-specific parts.

OPTION C: 15 QUESTIONS MODEL

Sometimes, I like to have a checklist for a project. In the 15 Questions Model, I brainstorm the questions you can ask to make sure your Translation Management Plan is complete regarding what materials to translate. Once you think through the questions, you will have more clarity on what you want to translate and how it fits into your plan.

Strategy:

1. Does multilingual communication and growth fit in with our strategic goals?
2. Do we have a Translation Management Plan?

Communications:

3. Will it raise our revenues or net earnings?

4. Are we missing any audiences, e.g., investors, shareholders, prospects, clients, employees?

5. Do we have defined content for the "buyer's journey"?

6. Can we measure the return of our investment on the translation?

7. Are our competitors translating?

8. Are our translations accessible (easy to find on the website)?

Risk:

9. Do we have any liability if we do *not* translate this content?

10. Does the translation need to be 100 percent accurate?

11. Does the law require us to translate this material?

Operations:

12. Can we simplify any processes by providing translated materials?

13. Do we have a clearly defined process for getting a translation?

14. Do we have a document management plan?

15. What resources do we have for procuring translation?

Whatever model you use for deciding what to translate, having a strategy and planning your original English content with translation in mind will set you up for higher returns on your multilingual marketing.

CONCLUSION

You have choices regarding who can do your translation. As with any purchase, you sacrifice quality and service when you opt for a lower price point. Consider your risk/return and make a Translation Management Plan so that your decision on who does your translation is clear.

A final suggestion: No matter who you use to do your translation, if it is important and can affect your bottom line, use a qualified editor! A professional editor is a fully bilingual and qualified translator. Appropriately trained and experienced translators and editors will provide you with a high-quality final document that you can trust.

In addition to using an editor, some clients like to have their translations reviewed by internal staff. We encourage that practice and do not charge extra for the original translator to incorporate any appropriate edits. Translation is like writing and a good internal reviewer likely will know appropriate company or industry terminology and understand company preferences. We do recommend that the company give guidance to employees on how to review a translation.

For recommendations on how to review a translation,
visit www.rapporttranslations.com/blog/how-to-proof-a-translation.

I hope that this chapter gives you clarity on how to find the best person to translate materials for you!

ACTION STEPS:

1. For quality assurance, use a professional translator to review any already completed translated materials, especially if done by nonprofessionals.

2. List out possible current translation resources and consider quality needs.

3. If you cannot hire a professional agency for everything, consider what hybrid model would help you get the quality you need.

CHAPTER 12

LESSONS LEARNED—HOW TO AVOID MISTAKES

"Bad communication ends a lot of good things."
—*Unknown author*

LESSON #1:

BILINGUAL PEOPLE WHO ARE NOT TRAINED TRANSLATORS MIGHT TAKE LIBERTIES WITH YOUR CONTENT.

My mother ran into a situation that gives us a good example of what can go wrong with translations.

The now retired Dr. Doris MacKenzie (a.k.a. Mom), traveled to China on a Fulbright Scholarship as a visiting professor from the University of Maryland a few years back. Needing some research documents translated, she turned to her bilingual research associate to translate the documents.

When it was done, she worried about the quality, so Dr. MacKenzie asked another one of her Chinese associates to *back translate* (take the Chinese documents and translate them back into English, a bit like the children's game "Whisper Down the Alley"). In a back translation, as in the game, the meaning can change through the different iterations. Luckily in this case, the back translation clearly illuminated that the translation did *not* match the English, at all.

Now, she had a Chinese translation that did not accurately capture her original English version. Dr. MacKenzie realized it was time to turn to me, her daughter and the owner of a translation firm, to ask how to proceed.

After teasing her about "you get what you pay for," we sent the original English documents and the Chinese translation to a professional translator who explained that the associate took many liberties with the translation to make it, in the associate's words, "more appropriate" for the Chinese culture. Professional translators never change a meaning unless they discuss the issue with the content writer or owner. When it is culturally inappropriate, they work together to develop an appropriate message. No author wants their message changed without knowing about it.

In this case, my mom had to pay two associates and a professional translator, not to mention wasted time following up on all this. From then on, she hired Rapport International, and of course, got the mom discount!

LESSON #2:

PROFESSIONAL TRANSLATORS TRAIN TO KNOW DIFFERENT WAYS TO CAPTURE MEANING AND WILL CONSULT WITH A CLIENT WHEN ANY QUESTION ARISES.

Our marketing department has loads of fun finding new words for our biweekly "Tidbits" email and social posts. We often find words in other languages that do not have a direct translation into English. Consider these great German words:

Kummerspeck: A term for excess weight gained from emotional overeating. It literally translates to "grief bacon" in English.

Katzenjammer: The German word for hangover, which literally translates to "cat's wail." Because, of course, hungover people sound like a wailing cat.

Schadenfraude: The feeling of happiness at the misfortune of others.

How about these words from other languages?

The Hawaiian phrase *pana po'o* refers to when one scratches their head while trying to remember something.

Jolabokaflod translates roughly to "Christmas book flood" and is a tradition in Iceland where people give books for presents on Christmas Eve.

After opening the presents people cozy up around the fire and read their new book.

"*Giving*" and "*Boom*" are examples of English words that caused challenges for our translators at Rapport International.

Giving: A client wanted to translate "giving" into 12 languages to put on a holiday greeting card. In English, we talk about the season of "giving," and it can stand alone, meaning to be generous. Translators across multiple languages said that it would not make sense without either a subject to go with the verb or a meaning attached.

Boom: Dan Tyre, the author of *Inbound Organization* loves to use the word "boom" when he trains HubSpot partners and salespeople. He uses "boom" in many situations, which, of course, presents difficulties in translation because no traditional meaning or translation exists for the word. Translators need to understand the context and work with the client to find the emotion and meaning that the client wants to portray.

Here are some examples of words that do not have a direct translation and different ways to handle the situation:

1. **Keep the word the same in the translation.** Dan Tyre uses the word "boom" to mean "good job," "I'm excited," "congratulations," "you did it," "I'm happy for you," "way to go," "good to see you." You get the idea. It is his signature happy word. The expression would need no translation. Even in character languages, the translator could keep it in the original English "boom." Translators do that for newly patented words or in situations to capture a new meaning. An example would be Volkswagen's word Fahrvergnügen, which was much catchier than saying "the pleasure of driving."

2. **Use another word or phrase.** For Kummerspeck, a translator who does not know the language might translate the word into "grief bacon," which would be inaccurate. Yet, at times, like in a medical communication, it might not be worth explaining the whole sentiment, it may be fine to say, "emotional eating."

3. **Explain it.** If we keep the same word, Kummerspeck, and put it in another context—say an editorial on differences in culture—the translator would use the word and then put the full explanation in parentheses.

LESSON #3:

AGENCIES DIFFER GREATLY, SO TAKE THE TIME TO FIND THE RIGHT ONE FOR YOU.

Not all agencies are created equal. Michelle Safrit of Conitex Sonoco learned that lesson. She came to us through their creative agency, a HubSpot partner that worked on creating their website. Prior to working with us, she hired a translation agency that provided poor-quality translations. At the beginning of the engagement, the agency did not disclose that they used machine translation with human editing. Luckily, Michelle is smart, and before submitting the whole project at once, she started them with a test project. From that sample, she found out that the quality did not meet her standards.

LESSON #4:

STICK WITH THE SAME TRANSLATOR FOR CONSISTENCY OF VOICE AND MESSAGE.

In 2004, when I purchased Rapport International from Lisa Gavigan, she told me a story about a client who started with her in 1987. The client sent all their packaging and user manual translations to Rapport International but, prior to a big convention, they wanted to get a large pricing catalog translated to use at their booth. They decided to get price quotes from different agencies and one agency cut their price to win the project.

At the convention, the salespeople found the catalog useless. Why? The product names did not match the names on the packaging. The other agency retranslated all the names differently, so the package names did not match the catalog names. Ever since then, the client has used our services for consistency and quality.

I know of competitors that assign any available translator to new projects. If consistency matters to you, make sure to hire an agency that provides linguistic matchmaking. The project managers at Rapport International take the time to assign the right translator to each new project. For subsequent projects from that client, the same translator gets assigned. We discussed linguistic matchmaking in Chapters 9 and 11.

LESSON #5:

DO YOUR MARKET RESEARCH BEFORE LAUNCHING A PRODUCT.

All over the internet there are examples of bad decisions and poor planning that led to embarrassing and unsuccessful launches of products and companies into foreign markets. Most of those issues could have been avoided by (a) doing a little market and brand name research prior to launch, (b) becoming familiar with the norms, culture, and slang of your new market, and/or (c) using an agency that could identify issues and make suggestions prior to launch.

Here are some well-known car company examples:

- When Mitsubishi marketed its Pajero in Spain, they were embarrassed to discover too late that Pajero is slang for "wanker" or "masturbator." I think it goes without saying that the men of Spain did not line up to purchase one.[38]

- American Motors also had trouble with a model name when they attempted to market the Matador in Spanish-speaking Puerto Rico. Instead of conjuring up images of strength and courage, the word matador translated into "killer."[39]

- Another car brand that had issues was Peugeot in China. In Mandarin, the spoken name of Peugeot, Biao Zhi, means "handsome," but in the dialect of southern China, Biao Zhi sounds like the word for "prostitute." Not Peugeot's desired image![40]

- It is not just translation that can go wrong. Fiat hired actor Richard Gere in advertisements for their Lancia Delta car, and the campaign created a storm in China. Richard Gere, a Dalai Lama follower, and supporter of Tibetan independence starred in the commercial that showed him driving to join a child dressed as a Tibetan monk. Fiat apologized to China who perceived the ads as pushing for political change about Tibet.[41]

Follow me on LinkedIn to get a steady stream of stories like these:
www.linkedin.com/in/wendypease/.

LESSON #6:

WRITE GOOD SOURCE CONTENT.

A professional translator works to keep your message accurate and in the same register (reading level) as the source or original content. When the author writes clearly and concisely, the translator has an easier time communicating the message.

Imagine getting this content to translate:

"I've got news for you all. We have had a rough year, as you know, but we have been recovering slowly but surely. But, of course, something had to mess up. Because Hank shipped three pallets to the wrong customer last week, the board has decided to update the shipping procedure for the entire loading dock.

This is something we will have to get used to, even if it wastes all our time in the process. Whenever we get an order ready to go, everyone on the loading dock will need to confirm shipments with me first. Only after I sign off on the details will anything be allowed on the shipping truck. This new change better prevents more careless errors."

This letter would be hard to translate because of the following:

1. Heavy use of passive tense. It is better to use subject and active verbs for clarity.

2. Many uses of unnecessary words such as "as you know" or "of course."

3. Unclear message. Is it about a rough year or about a new shipping procedure?

4. Run-on sentences.

It would be much easier to understand both in English and to translate if the author wrote the following:

"The board implemented a new shipping procedure because last week, we mistakenly shipped three pallets to the wrong customer. Although it may take more time, all shipments need my signature before they load onto the shipping truck. This change will avoid future mistakes."

If you take the time to craft well-written content, the translator will have an easier time capturing your message.

LESSON #7:

USE A TRANSLATOR WITH THE RIGHT STYLE AND EXPERIENCE.

Who writes your marketing content? My guess is that you never ask your engineers to write your website or packaging content. Yet, if you need technical documentation, you might ask your engineers to write it.

A client asked us to translate a spec sheet into Spanish. After we delivered the translation, the client asked their administrative assistant with high school training to review the translation. Our translator, who is a native Spanish-speaking professional with a PhD in International Studies, became annoyed with the edits made by the assistant because they contained grammatical errors and changes to the meaning. We took the feedback to the client and explained that the edits did not make sense.

When asking bilingual people to translate or review, consider their education, training, and experience. It matters.

LESSON #8:

ALLOW ENOUGH TIME.

We do get a chuckle when people ask us to do a 12-page translation for next day delivery. We like to ask, "How long did it take you to write, edit, and finalize the document?" In most cases, it took a week or two.

Translation takes about the same amount of time as it does to write content. It helps to realize that translators are grammar, writing, and communications experts. Just as a writer takes the time to craft a message in one language, the translator receives and then converts the message to another language. A good marketing translator continually watches for any cultural messages that will not connect with the audience. Thus prior to starting a project, we always want to know the audience and the use for the translation so we can communicate that objective to the translator.

Large, rushed projects risk not giving the translator enough time to think through the content just as a writer would.

In general, we suggest allowing for about 1,000 words per day. Although the translators can do more than that amount, the formula allows for clarifications and questions along the way.

LESSON #9:

AVOID IDIOMS.

How would you explain the following phrase? "Sliding in on a shrimp sandwich."

You probably have no idea what that expression means unless you speak Swedish and know that "Att glida in på en räkmacka" literally means "to slide in on a shrimp sandwich," and that the intended meaning is "somebody who didn't have to work to get where they are."

Interpreting idioms and sayings is a challenge for any professional linguist as they must understand the idiom and then accurately convey the message.

First, what is an idiom and who uses them?

Idiom: an idiom is an expression that takes on a figurative meaning when certain words are combined, which is different from the literal definition of the individual words.

There are thousands of idioms, occurring frequently in all languages and every language has its own collection of sayings. They can offer advice, transfer underlying ideas, principles, and values of a certain society, or be driven by trends, such as pop culture. Some common idioms in the US include:

- It is raining cats and dogs.
- If life gives you lemons, make lemonade.
- You hit the nail on the head.

Interpreting idioms can present some of the more challenging (and sometimes awkward) situations when communicating through a professional interpreter. Idioms will make no sense directly interpreted into a second (target) language. Or, worse, they will make literal sense but not in the way intended in the original (source) language. Idioms are woven in language and culture; their meaning and usefulness typically starts and ends with people who share the same language and cultural background.

The danger of misunderstandings in places, languages, and cultures is a big responsibility on the linguist to convey the intended meaning. An interpreter needs to capture the meaning and succinctly convey it, especially if no similar idiom exists in the target language.

Experts estimate that the English language has over 25,000 idioms.[42]

Native speakers of English use idioms all the time, often without realizing that they are doing so. When you create materials to be translated and used in other markets, refrain from using idioms. If you find yourself using one of the 25,000 English-language idioms, just remember that it is not "a piece of cake" to translate idiomatic expressions. And if you are trying to be creative "to make lemonade out of lemons," your friends in Nigeria will not understand. They will tell you that they prefer "to make pepper soup when life gives them peppers."

Now that you understand how to make lemonade *or* pepper soup, you can avoid common mistakes as you venture forth in your multilingual marketing. It is now time to turn our attention to specific considerations—starting with your website.

ACTION STEPS:

1. Review your content for quality and appropriateness for translation.

2. Edit any content in global English to avoid idioms, jokes, and local references.

3. Build an editorial calendar in your Translation Management Plan that allows time for translation.

CHAPTER 13

OPTIMIZE YOUR WEBSITE TO WIN GLOBAL SALES

*"It took me quite a long time to develop a voice, and now
that I have it, I am not going to be silent."*
—Madeleine Albright, 1st female US Secretary of State

There is no such thing as a <u>global language</u>! You can convert up to <u>three</u> times more website visitors into customers when you translate content into their native language.

Andrew White of Comptus has the distinguished honor of being the first accidental exporter that I encountered. Around 2007, I taught a class on global marketing at the New Hampshire Office of International Commerce. Andrew attended because he wanted to learn how to win business from the inquiries that he received from Germany.

Originally, he thought he had to translate his whole website to engage, but when I spoke with him after the class, I realized that he only wanted to sell five products in Germany. By limiting his translation to those five product pages and his "About Us" and "Ordering" pages, the translation project fit both his budget and his goals.

I call him an "accidental exporter" because he saw the international demand for his wind and environmental sensors and reacted, rather than having to create a plan, visit the country, do international trade shows, build a team, or find a distributor. He accidentally found a need for his products and took steps to export.

To read the case study about Comptus, visit
www.rapporttranslations.com/case_studies/comptus.

Remember the statistics mentioned in Chapter 4:

- 90 percent of people prefer to visit sites in their native language.
- 72.1 percent will spend more time on a site in their native language.
- 72.4 percent are more likely to buy on a site in their native language.
- 56.2 percent will spend more money if purchasing from a site in their native language.

The numbers show that buyers want information in their native language. Furthermore, access to international buyers skyrocketed with global access to the internet. In Chapter 1, I spoke about the benefits of global marketing. In this chapter, we will examine ways to translate your marketing outreach to bring buyers to you through digital marketing.

At this point in the book, whether you realize it or not, we have a framework for global inbound marketing. In the preceding chapters, we examined each area necessary to build the framework. Now, I will apply the framework by working through each of the areas—strategy, process, technology, and quality—to come up with a website translation plan that will work for you.

STRATEGY

While considering the strategy for your website, it is helpful to think about the site as a conversation. When a potential buyer arrives at your website, they have a question, and they want you to answer it. That exchange leads to another question for you to answer. When you translate your website, you want to think about those questions and how you are going to interact with the site visitor. When you understand that aspect, you can develop a strategy for your website translation.

(Of course, prior to this stage, you want to clarify your company and marketing strategies because your multilingual strategy needs to align with both.)

Here are two very different website strategies:

- Remember Joseph Gray from DRMetrix? He reached out to us because he had received email inquiries from different countries. His technology research company could provide services to non-English speakers, but the sales process was not able to answer the appropriate questions from prospects. He originally asked if we could translate email communications so he could respond to the questions. After hearing his goals, we suggested that he create a landing page with answers to the top questions he gets. It saved him money and time as the buyers could read the answers on the website.

- Let's revisit Conitex Sonoco too. It is a manufacturer of quality packaging materials. The company has international offices and sells different packaging in each location. Rather than a multinational approach where each country manages their own website, the company wanted a unified brand with local information for products and services. In addition, it has robust marketing activities and plans for regularly releasing appropriate content in each language. That requirement took a distinctive strategy. The team created content plans by country, language, and product, thereby allowing everyone to be clear on the multilingual communications strategy.

These two examples demonstrate how having a clear understanding of what the businesses wanted to accomplish helped them figure out their strategy.

Once you have a strategy, remember to set your goals so that you can measure how your website is performing. In Andrew White's case, he saw leads coming in from Germany and he wanted to increase them. His goal was SMART: specific, measurable, achievable, relevant, and timely. His goal was to increase inbound inquiries from German-speaking leads by 15 percent in the next six months.

PROCESS

The second step in translating your website is the process. If you develop a clean, clear process, you can replicate it for other languages or markets that you add in the future.

Framework: Start by knowing your website platform—it could be WordPress, HubSpot, Drupal, Wix, Squarespace, or another. Each platform has different abilities for handling translation. With this in mind, you want to decide whether to translate a mirror site, a micro-site (a smaller version of your full site), or a single landing page. You have options to start out slowly and increase your presence. Just remember to keep answering your visitors' questions.

Content: Once you decide on the framework, you need content for those pages. If you do a full mirror site, you already have the content. (We will discuss cultural adaptation in the next chapter to make sure your content is appropriate and resonates with your readers.) If you are doing a micro-site or landing page, you want to include: (a) a little about why you are different, (b) the benefits and features of what you are selling, (c) appropriate content on both pricing and how to order, and (d) testimonials or reviews.

Team: By defining key roles, you know who is responsible for each step. Internally, you need a person who understands the website strategy and marketing messages. That person can answer any questions and facilitate conversations with others involved. Refer to Chapter 11 for more details on picking a qualified translator.

Globalize or Localize: A prospect asked me if a general rule is to localize consumer products/services (business to consumer or B2C) and globalize business products/services (business to business or B2B). The answer depends on your strategy and budget.

If you sell soccer balls or footballs (futbols, as they are known in many parts of the world), your content probably needs to be localized. You benefit from showing local sports heroes, local references, and local teams. In Massachusetts, where I live, we want to see Revolution colors, logos, and players. Even if the Seattle Sounders are ranked Number One (as they are as I write this), content about that team will not catch my attention.

But if you sell raincoats for bicyclists, you are solving a problem that everybody understands. Images and references that make sense to all prospects are puddles, downpours, and the black line that bikers get up their back when riding through dirty water. You can start with globalized content until you decide that localized content might increase sales.

Upload: When the content is done, it is time to upload it to your website. Whoever does it must know the platform, know how to handle foreign fonts, and know how to navigate the site. Options include your webmaster, creative agency, or translation agency. No matter who does it, make sure you have a quality assurance check by the original translator to look for dropped text, appropriate line breaks, image displays, and working navigation.

Hint: At this point, it makes sense to mention accessibility. The Americans with Disabilities Act requires that websites of organizations that receive federal funding need to be accessible to those with disabilities. Section 508 gives the details for how to make websites accessible to the hard of hearing and visually impaired. If your site is 508 compliant for English, you might have to be compliant for any other languages.

Timing: If it takes three weeks to write the content, allow three weeks to translate the content. Translators are like writers. They need to craft the message so that it works in the target language and culture. While the content is being translated, the translation agency, webmaster, or creative agency can build the anticipated pages for the translation.

Updates: Websites are not static anymore. Experienced marketers consistently add new content to keep the search engines engaged with your site. Plus, you will likely find edits, changes, and additional content you will want to update. If you take the time to track these changes, you can develop a process for updating your translations.

Hint: At the start of the project, clarify your process so that everyone works off the same plan.

TECHNOLOGY

Once you outline your process, you can look at technologies that can simplify your efforts.

Build: You know what platform your website uses. With that information, you can determine how to set up the translations. If you do a landing page, you probably do not need to leverage much technology to upload the translation to the page. If you have a very robust website with lots of content that needs to be translated, technologies exist that automatically pull the original content from your website and send it to human translators. When the translator completes the project, the technology automatically places it back on your site. For example, WordPress has a plug in called WPML that works well.

Updates: Using the same technology for updates allows you to capture content changes. Some companies update infrequently, so they can just email the updates to us to translate. Others update regularly, so we use a different technology to receive automatic alerts when something needs to be translated and updated. A defined process saves their employees steps in gathering the content, submitting it, getting it back, and uploading it.

Since there are so many platforms and methods, we suggest you work with your translation agency to figure out the best process for you.

Navigation: The biggest mistake that I see on websites is hard-to-find access to translated content. It is best practice to put your language switcher (a globe icon) at the top right-hand side of your pages.

To learn more about navigation suggestions, watch the vlog at www.rapporttranslations.com/videos/website-navigation-translation-checklist.

Forgotten text: Do not forget to translate your headers and footers, buttons, calls to action, and navigation options. I see so many pages that have the content translated but look sloppy because other items are forgotten.

Hidden text: Titles, subtitles, page description, meta tags, etc., all need translation. Sometimes people forget about those items because they are not visible on the website. This is the information that search engines read, so make sure it is translated and optimized.

Techie stuff: Tags are cues that the website developers insert into websites to assist search engines in accurately finding your site. Inserting "hreflang" or "hrefcountry" tags identify the language or country of the visitor. The tags are signals to search engines on what language to display. You can find the full listing of the tags in the Resources section at the end of this book.

Sometimes companies that put in the language or the country code do not include the language switcher on the top of the page. I recommend that you keep the translation navigation front and center because if I speak English and I live in Argentina, I want to have the choice to navigate to the English page.

Cookies: Remember to set your cookies (visitor tracking) so that your website remembers that a visitor prefers the English content even though they live in Argentina. Many countries have regulations about inserting cookies, so translate your pop-up or header to allow for cookie capturing.

There are many books about the technology of website setup, search, and optimization. This chapter only highlights the key considerations of translated websites. In the next section, we go deeper into quality translation for your website as that subject is not often covered in depth in other books.

QUALITY

Your website is your public face. Quality counts here, and since the biggest fear of multilingual marketing is not knowing the language, let us eliminate that fear. By building a quality checklist, you can rest assured that your content says exactly what you want it to say in a culturally appropriate way.

1. **Hire the right translator:** Make sure the translator is professionally trained and experienced in your subject matter. By hiring the wrong person, you increase your risk of liability and accrue the extra expense of fixing problems later.

2. **Provide a glossary:** For company- and industry-specific terminology, keep a glossary of the terms and translations. Then, even if you change translators, you will not lose that consistency.

3. **Determine a review process:** If your material is highly technical or creative, best practice is to hire a professional editor who has the same qualifications as the translator. Or you might choose to have an internal, fully bilingual, and qualified employee or distributor review the translation.

4. **Finalize the content:** Prior to loading any content to the website, make sure the original translator and the reviewers agree on the final version. That way, you will know you have a good-quality translation.

5. **Create pages for the translation:** Be thoughtful about how you build the pages that hold the content. Make sure the build is aligned with your strategy.

6. **Build in thoughtful navigation:** Use a globe on the top right side of your screen to display the language options (and translate the languages so users can find theirs). People recognize the globe symbol as the standard for finding translation on a website.

7. **Load the content:** Appoint someone familiar with the language and/or with foreign language desktop publishing to load the content. They will pay close attention to detail so that all the content loads correctly.

8. **Check for cultural appropriateness:** Check that images, colors, pictures, and other visuals connect with your audience. Professional translators and editors will know to verify those elements. If you are unsure that they are checking for cultural adaptation, ask them to confirm this.

9. **Determine access:** Decide whether to show navigation to untranslated pages or not. Some companies know their audiences do

not want to see content that is not in their language. Leaving the pages in the navigation will look sloppy. Other companies know that their visitors speak enough English to show the English pages. Make sure you think through who your buyers are (see below for two examples).

10. **Check your contact information:** When visitors want to reach out to you, make it easy. Check your contact information to make sure it works in all markets. In Chapter 17, we will discuss how to handle incoming questions. Read about the many available options to facilitate multilingual communications before rushing to hire full-time bilingual staff for all the languages you encounter.

11. **Final review:** Have your initial translator review your translated web pages before final launch. The review includes looking for complete content, dropped text, appropriate spacing, paragraph breaks, and cultural appropriateness.

12. **Updates:** Prepare for updates. Consistency, attention, and use of technology keep your translated website current.

Regarding point number 9 on your quality checklist, here are two examples of real-world companies that decided to show untranslated content. In the first situation, not translating some content caused a problem. In the second situation, showing the original English navigation helped the company make future translation decisions.

Company One manufactures a heat-resistant paint used by engineers around the world. Visitors are not usually bilingual, and they want information about the heat tolerance of the paints. They want the specific information in detail so that they clearly understand it. Showing English content to these buyers does not help and might make them feel uneasy if they believe they cannot read important information. The company built a micro site that showcased just the products sold in each country and only offered translated copy on that site. On their main site, a buyer could navigate to the micro site without realizing it was shorter than the main site because the company carefully thought about the buyer's journey in each language and provided appropriate content.

Company Two markets medical products to engineers who understand some English because it is more commonly used in this industry. English is not their native language, so the company knows they can increase sales with translation. Prior to converting the whole site, they picked some pages to translate to measure success across the different languages. In this case, it was helpful to leave the website navigation in English to track what additional information the buyers wanted.

When we get a request to translate a website, at times people seem a little annoyed when we cannot give them a price without speaking to them. They do not understand that it is not as easy as grabbing a URL and spitting back a price. With thoughtful discussion and a clear strategy, their translated website can work the way they want it to without wasting time and money.

ACTION STEPS:

1. Add content to your multilingual marketing plan. Include the following:

   - Strategy: your company strategy, marketing strategy, and multilingual strategy.

   - Process: outline the key steps.

   - Technology: determine your needs.

   - Quality: list your materials and the quality needed.

2. Research various translation services to obtain the best provider for you.

CHAPTER 14

DRIVE MULTILINGUAL VISITORS TO YOUR SITE WITH SEO AND SOCIAL MEDIA

"Language is the road map of a culture. It tells you where its people come from and where they are going."
—*Rita Mae Brown, American feminist writer*

Think of the last networking event you went to. You probably walked in hoping to meet some good contacts and engaged in a lot of small talk that eventually led to more in-depth conversations. Those conversations ultimately closed deals.

I think of SEO and social media as a networking event. You "attend" and hope to meet the right people—for partnerships, business, referral sources, or professional friendships. Your website then becomes your dinner table. You invite the right people and deepen the conversation.

If you spend time preparing for in-depth conversations through your website, make sure you also network appropriately so that prospects can find you. In other words…

DO NOT IGNORE SEO. TRANSLATE IT!

Localizing and globalizing your website through translation helps you speak to the humans in your target market. Translating your SEO data helps you speak to the search engines in your target market. You may have an expertly translated website, but if your customers do not find you in their online searches, your efforts will be lost. Remember to translate all parts of your website, including keywords, expressions, tags, titles, anchor texts, script messages, image titles, and subtitles, so that search engines can find and rank you in the target language.

Much can go wrong when trying to optimize your SEO for global traffic. Country and language href tags (technical language on a website that tells the search engine that the content is in certain languages) can be complex and confusing; badly translated keywords can make your site unsearchable; having content duplicated too closely on each page can confuse search engines, and worse. Yet, if you have a plan set up from the beginning, you can manage it successfully.

OPTIMIZING YOUR WEBSITE
FOR SEARCH ENGINES

Here are nine key points for optimizing your website for global SEO. Much of this is quite technical, and I do not cover the necessary detail for you to implement this yourself. My purpose is to give you a strategic understanding so that you can ask the right questions about these issues when you hire a website professional, to make sure you find someone that understands multilingual SEO. A reminder from the last chapter: have your developer insert tags into your website to give language and/or location information to the search engines.

1. Develop a web page standard to use either the language or language/country codes on your website.

2. Use ISO standards for country codes to get them right. See the Resources section of this book for a link that shows the language and country tags.

3. Know who owns the responsibility of creating and updating your website's "hreflang" tags—either the webmaster or the marketing, technology, or localization department.

4. Make an "hreflang" plan to know whether you will have, for ex-

ample, a global Spanish for all countries or a separate tag for each country to account for currencies, local references, etc.

5. Create and make available a sitemap that is unique for each market/language.

6. Test your keywords and search phrases in the targeted markets. Make sure the results are culturally relevant and appropriate.

7. Maintain a keyword/search phrase glossary for each market/language and be consistent with those terms.

8. Measure the performance of your foreign language pages, by "hreflang" tag or URL, to see the difference in performance by country and language.

9. Leverage knowledge gained by reviewing measurements and adjust accordingly in other countries to increase success in every market.

TROUBLESHOOTING YOUR SEO PLAN

Now, if you find out that your SEO plan is not working as expected, here are the elements to investigate:

1. Relying on Google Translate to provide your website translation does nothing to assist your global SEO because Google recognizes it as machine-generated content, so your site will not show up as a search result in non-English markets.

2. Make sure your keywords are appropriately translated and culturally relevant. Are they what your target audience is searching for? If not, do more research.

3. Cookies could cause an issue. A person who accepts cookies in English might have difficulty getting to the in-language/country-specific page that is appropriate for them.

4. If you cloned your pages for different languages, the content might be too similar, which confuses search engines and could lead to the wrong language page showing up in results.

5. Sitemaps can cause issues if you have a page for each country but only made one map per language. Residents in many countries can speak the same language.

6. Transition from URL to "hreflang" tags. URLs built by language

can cause confusion for search engines. Updating your URLs to tags can help.

7. Webmasters can choose from more than 180 unique combinations of "href" language-country tags. Make sure they use the tags correctly on your website to target and measure results accurately.

8. "Hreflang" tags for language are required, but country is optional. Using only a language tag means you are globalizing for that language; using a language-country tag means that pages should be specific for both language and country (localized). Set up your pages correctly.

9. Make sure your "hreflang" tags are set up according to language first, then country, separated by a hyphen. Also, language tags are typically lowercase, and country uppercase, but having both in lowercase should not cause problems. Their order is the most important part.

10. "Hreflang" tags are not always intuitive. Look them up to ensure you are using the correct tag. For example, you might assume "sp" is for the Spanish language but the correct tag is "es." Or you might assume "UK" is the correct country tag for the United Kingdom but it is Ukraine. The United Kingdom is "GB."

11. Inconsistent use of language versus country code can cause issues. Know the language you are targeting, not just the country. For example, "PE" is the country of Peru but it is not the language. There is no "pe" language code, so a search engine will not understand if that tag is the only one you use.

On a side note, your US marketing team might not like the impact that globalizing has on your website! Once your multilingual SEO starts working, your English site likely will see a decrease in visitors as the number of visitors shifts toward the multilingual pages. For regional marketing teams, that difference can be a source of competition, but in a well-managed global marketing department, it is an opportunity to share best practices.

SOCIAL MEDIA

Bill Gates once wrote that "Content is King."[43] He knew early on that websites with good content would attract readers. Marketers subsequently added that "Consistency is Queen," since search engines and people want a continuous stream of good content. I say that "Translation is the Princess," because if the content is in the person's native language, it will attract and hold their attention. Your king, queen, and princess apply to your website and to social media.

To watch a video with more about the princess, visit www.rapporttranslations.com/videos/translated-content-increases-lead-generation.

Consider social media as a business cocktail party where you do not know anyone. Of course, you dress appropriately, smile, start conversations with ice breakers, speak clearly, and add valuable insight. If you are engaging and interesting, people will want to get to know you. Likewise, on social media, you can attract the people with whom you want to engage by displaying the correct mix of interesting content, catchy images or videos, appropriate keywords, and by always engaging with people who comment on your posts. From there, you can invite prospects to dinner—that is, to your website—to have a deeper conversation.

Now, if you attend a networking event in another country, you will think about what the social norms and expectations are. It is the same for global social media posts. Most of the time, slight modifications to your plan will attract your target audience. By having a clear editorial calendar with planned posts, you can manage your multilingual posts.

Here are suggestions on how to adapt your social engagement:

1. **Create content that works globally.** Plan to capture global rather than local attention.

2. **Have a clear editorial calendar.** Know which posts will be adapted for each market.

3. **Time the release on schedule.** Watch for holidays and events in countries to maximize return.

4. **Customize posts for specific markets.** Look for special content that might draw extra attention.

5. **Be edutaining.** Educate while you entertain to capture people's attention.

6. **Be consistent.** Be there to be noticed.

7. **Research key words.** Use key words consistently across your social and web content.

8. **Use key words to point visitors to your in-language content.** Engage in more depth on your website.

Most importantly, track your website activity. If you know what pages, blogs, and information attract visitors who click through and stay, you can create more of that type of content to draw in prospects and to engage your audience.

Creating and posting content consistently can be challenging. Having an editorial calendar can keep you on track. At Rapport International, we have a shared calendar so that we know what we are posting each month. The calendar includes content for blogs, website updates, and social posts and follows a posting pattern to keep us on track.

This is the pattern that we use:

> Monday: Global Minute
>
> Tuesday: random language or culture information
>
> Wednesday: *The Global Marketing Show* podcast episode release
>
> Thursday: company-specific blog or update
>
> Friday: Fun Fact

We recommend these actions:

1. **Adapt the calendar.** Pick which posts are appropriate for each market. If you do not sell a product there, do not translate those posts. Or, if you want to focus on a special market opportunity, plan for it.

2. **Lag the translation release.** One month, the post is presented in English. During that month, the content is translated so that the translated version is ready to be posted the next month. January's English calendar for posts becomes February's calendar for the posts of translated content. The lag allows time to launch in English and then prepare the translation for launch the following month. The rolling process gives you time to adapt and launch on schedule.

3. **Track performance.** See what works across all markets and what might work better in different areas.

As you can see, with a little advance planning, you can adapt your networking conversations across languages and attract the right people to your dinner table. From there, you can continue to build relationships and delight your clients, no matter what language they speak. In Chapter

17, we will look at how to connect with clients in other ways to keep the relationship strong.

ACTION STEPS:

1. Assess your current SEO and search phrases to see if they are working and current.

2. Consider whether language or country "href" tags make sense for your business.

3. Explore whether your webmaster or translation agency is better equipped to handle your multilingual website.

4. Set up your social media calendar.

CHAPTER 15

BEST PRACTICES FOR VIDEOS, PACKAGING, USER INTERFACES, AND MORE

"Be faithful in small things because it is in them that your strength lies."
—*Mother Teresa*

U p until now, we have focused on how to get the translations you need. Once you have a clear plan, a time will come when your translations need to work in a variety of different formats. In this chapter, I will discuss some of these special situations so that you know how to handle them.

VIDEO

What do you do with your videos so that people understand them?

Videos are a great form of engagement and are frequently added on websites and in social marketing. Yet, companies that translate content and leave the videos in English miss out on "speaking" to their audience in the right language. You spent time and money creating great videos, now have them reach your audience.

Here are the two choices for translating your videos:

1. **Add translated subtitles at the bottom:** Doing subtitles is a less expensive option, especially if you already have a written script

and you do not need to pay to transcribe it. Once you have an English script translated, putting the subtitles into the video is just a simple edit. Subtitles might look the same but are not the same as close captioning, which uses a slightly different technology and provides text for deaf and hard-of-hearing audiences. Sometimes the terms are used interchangeably but they are different. Close captioning includes descriptions of music, sounds, and background noise. Subtitles provide just the spoken words since the audience can hear the sounds. In this chapter, I talk about subtitles because I am writing about language understanding.

2. **Do a voice-over:** A voice-over would entail translating the script, hiring native-language voice talent, recording the script, and then dubbing the recording over the video.

Both are good options depending on the use of your video. Voice-overs have a few extra steps but might be worth it, depending on your audience.

SUBTITLES VERSUS VOICE-OVERS

Subtitles work well for:

- International audiences who regularly read subtitles on Hollywood movies.

- Limited budgets because there is no need to hire voice talent.

- Messages intended for professionals who might "work" a little harder for access to the information.

- Highly visual videos because the person will be watching the screen already.

- Training videos where the audience must watch with full attention.

Consider your specific audience, but keep in mind that people now tend to watch videos on mute, therefore subtitling is popular.[44]

Consider any limitations of your audience: people who are blind or have low vision or those with difficulty reading appreciate dubbing, while those who are deaf and hard of hearing prefer subtitles.

In addition, think about the reading skills of the people watching your videos. Someone who has difficulty reading will have more difficulty keeping up with subtitles.

SPECIALTY LAYOUTS

Occasionally, we receive calls from printers asking if we can prepare print-ready translated brochures for their clients. Their clients seem to think that the printer presses a button on their printing equipment and the brochures automatically change languages.

Printers know that creating content and a layout for a brochure takes time before it can be printed. There is no "easy button" to convert a brochure into another language. Printers partner with companies like Rapport International for translation and layout.

For the brochure, a monolingual copy writer with subject matter expertise, the right voice, and style writes the content. After that is complete, a fully bilingual translator who also understands the subject matter and has the right voice and style does the translation. Both the writing and the translation take roughly the same amount of time.

Then, the brochure needs a layout, which requires a creative person who has training in layout programs, colors, images, sizing, spacing, and the ability to visualize a pleasing design appropriate for the material. Normally, the designer is not the person who completes the foreign language layout.

Specialists called foreign language desktop publishers (FLDTP) have specific skills to lay out foreign language materials accurately. FLDTP professionals pay more attention to process and accuracy than to creativity. They focus on replacing the original text with the translation and adapting the original layout to accommodate the new text, which can involve resizing the elements to fit in the same space, adapting fonts so they display accurately, and placing complete text in the right format.

An experienced FLDTP knows all the same design programs that a single-language designer knows, plus has knowledge about languages and foreign fonts. In addition, she understands various cultures and acts as another set of eyes on the content to check for appropriate colors, visual references, or content presentation.

Rapport International's specialist speaks five different languages! With her language abilities, layout skills, and attention to detail, she excels in foreign language layouts, but she does no original design work. This is the type of person you want to handle your foreign language layouts.

PREPARING MATERIALS FOR FOREIGN LANGUAGE PUBLISHING

If you are creating a brochure, user manuals, package inserts, PDFs, or other visual materials and you know the material will be available in multiple languages, you can take steps in advance to make sure that the material will work well in other languages.

Use simple design elements. Avoid embedded text in graphics that will need to be translated into the new language. This will cause longer turnaround times because the FLDTP will need to pull the text out and redesign the item for the new language. Also, keep things simple because design elements might have to move around to make the layout work.

Leave space. When you translate from one language into another, the translation can be up to 30 percent longer and will therefore need more space. A Finnish word that is starting to take hold in the US is kalsari-kannit (pronounced cal-sar-y-cuhn-eet), defined as "the feeling when you are going to get drunk home alone in your underwear with no intention of going out." With no equivalent word in English, it is an extreme example to show that a translation can be more than 30 percent longer.[45] FLDTPs appreciate a designer who builds in extra white space that allows for expansion.

Do not start the layout until the copy is finalized. Let me say it again: Do *not* send the project to the FLDTP until the copy is translated and finalized. If you start doing the layout with outstanding translation edits, you will end up with issues regarding version control and messaging. Compounding that mistake across multiple languages creates a real mess. Wait until you have finalized the translation before you send it to your FLDTP.

Plan ahead. Finally, you need to plan enough time for the FLDTP process; it is not as simple as pulling out the original language text and dropping in the translated text. The process of inserting, formatting, fitting the text, *and* ensuring the cultural appropriateness of the colors, images, graphics, and layout takes time. FLDTPs will provide a timeframe for completion once they assess the original layout.

Use common fonts. If the designer chooses a font that does not exist for the new language, the FLTDP will have to change the font in the entire document, which could change the look and feel. In addition, some fonts do not have the special characters needed in some languages, such as accents, tildes (ñ), or letters such as ü in German or æ in French. Make sure that the chosen font will handle all the characters.

Be aware of punctuation differences. The way languages hyphenate varies. Make sure that if a layout uses hyphens, that it breaks at the right place for other languages. Punctuation can vary as well. In Greek, a semicolon is a question mark. Quotation marks look different across languages. An experienced FLDTP knows these differences and makes sure that they are correct in the new language.

Use italics sparingly. Some languages do not use italics. If your designer uses italicized text for emphasis, your FLDTP will know which languages do not use italics and to emphasize the text in a different way.

Adjust numbers/currency. In the US, we use a comma in larger numbers, and a decimal point before decimals/cents. In some languages, the opposite is true. Your FLDTP will know the audience and will watch for the numbers being presented in a way that is culturally appropriate. For example, if the project is being translated for a Spanish-speaking audience in the US, the FLDTP will keep the numbers in the standard US convention, but if the material is for an international audience, they will make sure the numbers display appropriately.

Adapt visuals. Colors have a real effect on how an audience receives information. Colors have different meanings in different cultures. Remember how I mentioned that white symbolizes purity and brides in the United States while in China white means death. In China, red means happiness, joy, and excitement, in India it denotes purity, and in Japan it can mean danger. If your project uses color in a big, bold way, your FLDTP will advise you if they believe it could be interpreted differently in the other culture. They will suggest the most strategic way to handle color and image issues.

Display languages correctly. Languages like character languages or those that read right to left bring their own set of challenges. An experienced FLDTP will make sure that your project lays out correctly so that it makes sense when the audience is reading it. Sometimes, the FLDTP will have to change some of the layout or elements to make sure that it meets cultural expectations.

If you are a creative designer whose project might need to be translated into a more complex language, make sure that you do not group a lot of elements tightly together. Make the layout more flexible so that when the FLDTP substitutes the other languages, they can move elements around and make everything fit in a culturally appropriate way.

So, the question is, "Can your designer do your foreign language desktop publishing?" Some can, some cannot. As mentioned above, FLDTPs do not typically create, instead they focus on the details of adapting the materials from one language to another. If you are a creative specialist who is not familiar with languages and cultures, you might want to leave this process to the professional FLDTP. In the long run, you will save time, costs, and potential liability. On the other hand, if you are bilingual and you understand and feel comfortable with the culture of the target audience, sure, go for it. Just make sure that you have your translator review it.

> If you are interested in learning more about Arabic, a script that reads right to left, visit www.rapporttranslations.com/ blog/10-tips-for-english-to-arabic-translation.

FORMS

Sometimes, clients hire an interpreter to come in and help a customer fill out forms. That can work, but it is both cumbersome and expensive to schedule and pay an in-person or telephone interpreter every time you have a client who needs assistance completing forms.

A better alternative is to translate the forms into the languages you need most frequently. The benefit is that you translate them once and then you have them for every client who speaks that language, which also eliminates the need to schedule an interpreter each time. In the long run, you will save money.

In addition to following all the advice for the layout, fillable forms have a few other tricks to make them easier to use when translated.

Write in the right register. Every audience has an expected reading level, known as a register. When you write your forms in a register understandable to your audience, the translator keeps the material in the same register. This allows all your users to understand your forms, regardless of which language they read it in.

Use clear wording. We have all read a form with ambiguous questions. Ambiguity is painful. Do not use words or phrases that are unclear or could have a double meaning. It makes translation difficult and results in time spent seeking clarification, or worse yet, the meaning is misunderstood by the person filling out the form.

Offer multiple choice questions. Multiple choice questions give you responses that will not need additional translation, whereas open-ended questions will need the answers to be translated into English for you to understand the response.

Allow extra space in layout. Do not start with an overcrowded English form because you will have a real problem when you translate it. We talked about translation expansion before; that issue becomes very important on forms because you want people to be able to read and respond easily. Lack of space on a form is challenging for the responder.

Think about accessibility. Consider whether you going to use paper or electronic forms. If you plan to use electronic forms either in your office or on the internet, you need to make sure that you provide clear navigation. Customers will be more apt to comply with instructions and to complete the information when it is easy to follow. Make sure that the navigation is translated, easy to follow, and leads to information in the correct language.

PACKAGING TRANSLATION

Years ago, my father told me a story about a Chinese work associate who moved to the US with his wife. On their first visit to the grocery store, they picked out what they thought was going to be a nice dinner of fried chicken. The container had a picture of fried chicken on it, after all. To their surprise, when they got home and opened it up, they found a pile of Crisco instead.

In China, pictures on the packages show what is inside. In the US, the picture on the Crisco tub showed what you could make with the fat inside the container.

Reaching new markets successfully, avoiding liability, meeting regulatory requirements, and projecting a professional impression are all reasons to carefully develop clear, clean packaging.

Here are some points to remember:

White space: Packaging translation has its own special challenge because of the limited space for multiple languages. Take, for example, medical products. The packages already contain a lot of information: ingredients, descriptions, warnings, directions, side effects, symbols, and company branding. Any of those words in English could be three or more words in another language, which makes content layout on the package a major consideration.

Consistency: The information included on the package has probably already been used on catalogs, websites, advertising copy, spec sheets, and in other places. Keeping the translation consistent helps your audience identify your product faster. I am surprised at the number of times I have heard about company information not being consistent.

Regulations: Some countries require dual-language packaging. Canada, for example, requires all mandatory information on food labels be shown in both French and English. Make sure to meet country requirements when launching products in new markets.

Opportunistic packaging: While the US does not require bilingual packaging, many companies create North American packaging with English, Spanish, and French to access the US Spanish-speaking market as well as for Mexico and French for Canada. Those companies attract new customers and see revenues increase just by adapting packaging in their local market.

CE mark: This symbol, which says the product meets the requirements for safety, performance, health, and environmental protections, must be on certain products in the European market. The CE mark must be translated into the local language. Many companies find that if they get the CE mark, packaging, and user materials translated into all the European languages from the start, it is easier to expand when they are ready.

To read more about packaging translation visit
www.rapporttranslations.com/blog/packaging-translation-3-3-15.

SOFTWARE LOCALIZATION

USER INTERFACE (UI) AND USER EXPERIENCE (UX)

Software as a service (SAAS), direct ordering, global internet access, and demand for good software programs/apps that are translated for local users drive consumers worldwide to buy online. By providing a user interface (UI: what your customers see) and a user experience (UX: how your customers feel) adapted for your target customers, you will find it easier to move leads through the buyer's journey. Remember that consumers are more apt to buy (and spend more) if your content is in their native language and your site feels comfortable to them.

My number one recommendation is to make sure you build your platforms to accommodate multiple languages *from the start*. Too many times, we have seen platforms built for one language cause issues with translation/localization later when trying to expand internationally. Building your platform, the right way, from the start allows you to expand easier.

How to build your software for multiple languages is beyond the scope of this book because there are too many platforms and technologies to cover. Just know that the platform you choose is a key element to your success, even if you do not plan on translating now.

If your platform is not built for multiple languages, you can still localize it, but the process will be manual and cost more.

Platforms built for multiple languages have options for translation:

1. **Direct access for translators.** We have worked with clients who have their programs set up in a table format for language fields and want the translator to go directly in and add the translation. Once the language fields are populated, the client can make the system live for us to do a quality check on the interface. A translator with technology experience and subject matter expertise makes that step easy.

2. **Export and import.** Other clients prefer to export the content into a table format for the translator to populate. With the completed translation, they can import it back into their platform themselves.

3. **Application Programming Interface (API).** API technology allows two programs to talk to each other. We have an API that automatically connects to some programs and allows us to pull the content into our translation platform. Once the translation is done, we push it back onto the program.

When you develop your Translation Management Plan, part of your discussion should include technology. By thinking about your needs in advance, you save headaches later when you expand multilingually.

CONCLUSION

In *The Global Marketing Show* podcast (www.theglobalmarketingshow.com/) and in research with product managers, I hear about avoidable mistakes.

The number *one* mistake is not being consistent with naming and terminology. If you have one translator for your marketing materials, another doing the user interface (UI), and a third doing the software commands, they might all use a different translation for a single word.

Just think about it. Say I call the evening meal "dinner," you call it "supper," and our friend calls it the "evening meal." A non-native speaker is bound to be confused without enough information to know that all three terms refer to the same meal. This is a simple example, but I hear about terminology confusion all the time.

By coordinating your translation efforts, having naming protocols, and maintaining a glossary, your translations will be consistent and easier for your clients, prospects, and buyers across all your platforms and content.

ACTION STEPS:

1. Identify your key videos and add subtitles/voice-overs.

2. Assess the content that you identified for translation for layout readiness.

3. Review customer touch points to make sure translation supports all stages.

CHAPTER 16

CULTURAL ADAPTATION TO ENGAGE YOUR AUDIENCE

"Growth and comfort do not coexist."
—Ginni Rometty, CEO, IBM

D o you say "jimmies" or "sprinkles"?
"Scallions" or "green onions"?
"Soda," "pop," "soft drink," "tonic," or "coke"?
In any translation, a professional considers more than just the words and their meaning. Cultural norms and practices, pictures, colors, references, and presentation affect the appropriateness of the message too. For fun, look at pictures of people from around the world and see if you can guess if they are native to your country; chances are that you can probably guess which people are or are not from your country. People pick up on subtleties, and when you provide language translation, you want to make sure your message and its context are also appropriate.

More and more frequently, potential clients are asking about cultural appropriateness. They will ask, "Do you make the translation right for the audience?" or "Will it be right for the culture?" Immediately, I know that they must have knowledge about translation if they know to ask about cultural adaption, even though they might not know the correct terms.

Before we delve into how to "culturally adapt" materials, I want to refresh your memory of some terminology, so that we are all on the same page.

- **Translation** is the general term for converting written content from one language to another.

- **Globalization** is a type of translation where one good translation works for all parts of the world where that language is spoken. For example, Spanish can be used in Spain, Peru, Chile, and many other countries.

- **Localization** is a more targeted translation. With localization, every facet of translated material must work in a specific geography, culture, or community. For example, in France, prices would be shown in Euros.

- **Cultural adaptation** is making sure your translations, whether globalized or localized, are culturally appropriate for your audiences.

- **Transcreation** is creating marketing materials from scratch that are appropriate for culture and language. Transcreation is useful if no original marketing material exists.

Whenever a prospect calls with a potential project, we need to know where the translation will be used. Once we have that answer, we have a better understanding of how to provide a culturally adapted translation. While we work on the project, we look for any element that might prevent the translation from being culturally appropriate.

A picture is worth a thousand words. Graphics, screenshots, and photographs always need to be reviewed for appropriateness. A reviewer needs to check for models of the same race or culture, locations in the region, appropriate animals, and numbers. When prospective customers see an image, you want to make sure it gets a positive reaction. For example, a photo of a woman scientist with her hair tied in a ponytail while she uses a microscope might be offensive in a Muslim culture where women are expected to wear headscarves.

Colors. The choice of color carries significant meanings across cultures. For example, in the US, yellow is cheery and happy, while in China, yellow is associated with pornographic material. In France, yellow signifies jealously, betrayal, weakness, and contradiction. Be aware that colors have very different associations and meanings across the world. Read more about what colors mean in various cultures: www.huffingtonpost.com/smarter-travel/what-colors-mean-in-other_b_9078674.html.

Keep your jokes to yourself. Humor, idioms, colloquialisms, and pop culture terms do not translate well. Avoid them as they might cause confusion, or worse, be offensive to others.

Test brand names and slogans. Braniff Airlines wanted to promote their upgraded leather seats to their Spanish-speaking markets using the same slogan that they were using in the US: "Fly in Leather." The slogan did fine throughout most of Latin America, but in Mexico, the translation "Vuela en Cuero" gave a very different connotation. In Mexican Spanish, it meant "Fly Naked." While "Fly Naked" is memorable, it was not the intended message. Testing in each of the markets before the launch would have avoided this big gaffe.

"Untranslateable" word strategy. At times, writers use creative words, made-up words, or words with no translation in the target language. When certain words cannot be translated, you can leave the word in the original English, make up a new word in the language, or use multiple words to present the meaning. For example, a client Mach49 uses "Disrupting InsideOut™" to describe their work guiding global businesses to build a pipeline and portfolio of disruptive new ventures. They developed this tagline to talk about how the client's internal team can create a disruption or new way of thinking rather than looking to outsiders to bring innovation. That catchphrase is unique positioning for them, so we worked with their marketing lead and the translator developed in-language terminology to convey the message.

To read more about how to handle difficult words, visit www.rapporttranslations.com/blog/professional-translation-services-for-evolving-language.

Drop concepts that do not work. As good as a campaign might be, sometimes, it just does not work in another culture. Pepsodent launched a campaign to whiten teeth in Asia where many locals like to chew betel nut which blackens their teeth. No one cared about the promise to whiten teeth.[46]

Avoid references that do not make sense. When I interviewed Randi Roger about global marketing, on a great episode of *The Global Marketing Show* podcast (www.theglobalmarketingshow.com/e/english-not-the-global-language/), she spoke of a campaign that they developed in the US and sent to Japan for translation and launch. The message spoke about "providing a better customer experience." The Japanese marketing professionals explained that such a campaign would not work in Japan because their focus is solely on the customer experience, so they would never talk about improving it. It was a great campaign in the US but void of meaning in Japan!

Present your content appropriately. Years ago, we had a client who asked us to translate an informational brochure from English into Spanish. We did the translation, and the client asked their Spanish creative agency to review it. The creative agency came back with many edits and said that the changes were more culturally appropriate. The translator reviewed the edits and said that they changed the meaning. The client felt stuck in the middle because they did not know the language. To solve the issue, I suggested that we talk and resolve each change. On the call, it became clear that the creative agency made changes that were not wrong, they just conveyed a different message. The client got clear on the edits and decided on which version to use. Since they were in a regulated industry and needed to retain approved messaging, they decided to approve our translations as we carry a liability insurance policy on our quality.

Understand decision-making in the culture. In the US, we pride ourselves on independence and individual decision-making. In other countries, decisions are made in a group. The cultural terms for such differences are "individualism" and "collectivism." Be aware of cultural differences in decision-making and respect in your materials. For example, in Japan a Rotary International photographer took a picture in which the leader was seated lower than others. The image was inappropriate because in Japan, the leader always sits highest. It is a subtle and important distinction in Japan. The US team wanted to use the picture, thinking it was not a big deal. Luckily, their cultural advisors spoke up strongly enough that they took another picture. What might seem inconsequential in one culture can send a huge message in another.

Be aware of equality and inequality. Watch for conscious and unconscious bias across cultures. Check out companies' leadership teams. I am surprised at the number of companies that still have all White men in leadership positions. BCG research shows that, "Companies that reported above-average diversity on their management teams also reported innovation revenue that was 19 percentage points higher than that of companies with below-average leadership diversity—45 percent of total revenue versus just 26 percent." Companies with diverse leaders contribute to decisions that attract diversity and thus, more buyers.[47]

Think of friends and family. I once spoke with a woman who opened a yoga studio in a predominately Hispanic area of the US, and she had trouble getting the women to attend. As we discussed it, the reason became clear to me: Hispanic women want to be fit and do yoga, but they also value family time and relationships. I suggested that she make it family yoga classes. Subtle adjustments can make a big difference.

Understand faith, fact, or feeling. Some people believe the Almighty will lead them to the right decision, others listen to their feelings, and others base their decisions on facts. With two parents as professors, I learned to look at research and facts. If I want to buy a new product, I want to know the facts about it. My friend Morning Star needs to "feel" any decision that she makes. She looks for a gut reaction to it. It comes back to knowing your audience. To reach them, you want to know if they are looking for facts, an emotional reaction, or a sign from the Almighty.

Be aware of holidays. Speaking about celebrating the Fourth of July in the US is a great way to market products, yet not so big in the UK. Diwali in India is huge, as is Chinese New Year in many parts of the world, but those celebrations are not official holidays in the US. When writing content that will be translated, make sure to avoid referencing specific holidays or adapt the text for each location.

Money, money, money! Of course, if customers can buy your product online, you want to provide prices in local currencies. Maybe not so obvious, though, is that people's attitudes towards money vary. In some parts of the world, it is not bad manners to ask a person how much they make or how much their belongings cost, but in the US, such questions can be considered offensive. Be aware of how money appears in your content.

Although the challenges seem complex, culturally adapting materials is easy for a professional translator. Since they only translate into their native language, they will naturally notice "off culture" remarks, references, and mistakes. Be open to the conversation about cultural appropriateness and encourage your translator to bring any observations and suggestions to you. That way, you can make sure your materials are culturally appropriate for your intended audience.

ACTION STEPS:

1. Review your images, graphics, website, and visuals for diversity.

2. Think about what you can do to increase the diversity, equity, and inclusion on your team.

3. Look at your current clients to see how diverse they are.

CHAPTER 17

DELIGHTING CLIENTS DURING THE INEVITABLE GLOBAL BOOM

"Language is power, in ways more literal than most people think.
When we speak, we exercise the power of language to transform reality.
Why don't more of us realize the connection between language and power?"
—Julia Penelope, American linguist, author, and philosopher

My Great Uncle Art and Great Aunt Elsie took a tour through France while I was backpacking through Europe. Fortunately, I had the chance to meet up with them in Paris and Uncle Art had me in hysterics with his attempts to speak French. Our trip was before easy access to machine translation apps and accessible directions on smart phones, so Uncle Art had been pulling out his phrase book, studying, and practicing the words.

He was very proud of his newfound ability to ask directions. At one point, he got up the nerve to approach a local and ask, "Où est le Louvre?" He was so excited to be able to say it! Yet, when the person answered… Uncle Art had no idea what he said. He grinned and replied, "Merci," but he was still totally clueless about how to get to Le Louvre museum!

Inbound marketing can feel a bit like that conversation. You put your content out in other languages, but what happens when they respond?

Unfortunately, many customer service representatives hit "delete" on emails that are not in English. Instead of deleting, look for inquiries in foreign languages and provide resources for your employees to respond. You have options on how to handle multilingual communications besides hiring a multilingual person. Hiring for your company culture and matching it to the experience and ability of a person can be hard, not to mention requiring the right bilingual capabilities. And if you hire for one language, what about inquiries from all the other possible languages? A better option is to work with a language services company like Rapport International to support your multilingual engagement.

In Chapter 1, I spoke about the incredible opportunities for your business just by having an online presence. Since your content can reach the whole world, you want to connect to prospective buyers, no matter where they are located or what language they speak. So, how do you staff up for handling all language inquiries and client relationships?

Professional language services companies offer multiple ways to handle connections across languages without you hiring bilingual employees. For example, in Chapter 10, you read about DRMetrix, the technology research company that got emails in Chinese asking about their services. The owner asked us to translate the email inquiries and responses, but after talking about the process, we agreed that creating a landing page with translated FAQs solved his challenge. That alternative saved him money and leveraged translations for multiple uses.

Here are some other ways to connect across languages:

Provide information for the complete buyer's journey. In Chapter 10, we talked about what content to translate. If you are thoughtful about creating information in each stage of the journey and translate the most frequently used content across each stage, you will answer most questions that prospects might have. With a defined buyer's journey and properly translated content, prospects can buy directly, eliminating the need for more expensive translation or interpretation.

Pros:
- Answer questions in the consumer's native language.
- Track visitors by language and content.
- Enable visitors to buy online.
- Minimize time needed for in-person responses.

Cons:
- Takes thoughtful planning for the content needed.
- Needs well-written, quality translation.

- Unable to "wing it" or personalize answers.

- Lose customization for high-value prospects.

Implement live chat. Answering incoming inquiries through chat is more popular than ever, and consumers are driving this trend. Rather than call and wait on hold for answers, people like to chat online. It is efficient for both sides. Consumers can multitask as they get answers, and chat reps can look up answers and handle multiple conversations at once. By hiring bilingual chat representatives or outsourcing for these services as you would for a call center, it becomes simple to handle questions in multiple languages.

Pros:

- Engage with prospects in their preferred format and language.

- Access answers before responding.

- Hire across time zones for round-the-clock coverage.

- Outsource for part-time chat representatives.

Cons:

- Need bilingual personnel.

- Requires representatives to have full training.

- Must have a database of questions and answers.

Utilize chatbots. To really leverage your translations and technology, consider chatbots. If you know: (a) your top 10 customer support questions, (b) your top three most used business offerings, and (c) you have clearly defined your buyers' triggers, consider using automated responses on your chat. Once you write the content in English, you can translate the responses into the other languages you want to support.

Pros:

- Thoughtful scripting leads to great success.

- Easy to translate once scripting is done in English.

- Access at all hours.

- Relatively inexpensive.

- Program the chatbot to recognize the visitor's language to deliver responses in their preferred language.

Cons:

- It is not personal.
- Only answers previously defined questions.
- May not be able to understand the question.
- Possible trouble identifying the language.

Try telephone interpreting. This service is ideal for speaking with a prospect or client over the phone. With access to over 200 languages and 24/7 coverage, you can connect with an interpreter at all hours, so time zones do not matter. The interpreters are fully screened, tested, and recorded for training purposes. Telephone interpreting is a more dependable and professional option than asking on social media for a bilingual person to assist.

Pros:

- Great for on-demand, quick calls.
- Good for conference calls and customer service questions.
- Only pay for usage.
- No minimum charges.
- Efficient for call centers.
- Over 200 languages available.

Cons:

- No visual or body-language cues on a phone call.
- Confusing for the interpreter with a group.
- Not as personal as face-to-face meetings.

Institute video remote interpreting (VRI). For a more personal and visual connection, video remote interpreting (VRI) might be the right choice in certain situations. With VRI, all participants are in the same physical room except for the interpreter who connects through a secure video service. As with telephone interpreting, VRI services offer trained, experienced interpreters in many languages and can connect on demand. Using a video connection gives the interpreter the advantage of being able to see and read nonverbal, visual cues during the conversation, and the participants can interact visually. VRI requires an account and a device (computer, tablet, or phone) with a camera and internet connection. VRI is different from video meeting (or Zoom/Skype/Google Meet) interpreting, which I discuss in the next section.

To learn more about using VRI, visit www.rapporttranslations.com/blog/10-video-remote-interpreting-vri-questions-answered.

Pros:

- Gives an on-demand alternative to scheduled, in-person interpreting.

- Enhances personal connections while using technology.

- Shows facial expressions and other visual cues to improve accuracy of interpretation.

- Access on short notice.

- Offers more languages because the pool of interpreters comes from a wider geography.

- Saves costs over in-person interpreters with shorter time minimums and no travel expenses.

- Offers HIPAA-compliant, completely secure, and confidential connections.

Cons:

- Access to the interpreter is only on video, so the prospect or client must be in the room with you.

- Connection or power could fail.

- Must meet minimum requirements for internet speed.

- Lag in connection could affect the flow of conversation.

- The interpreter has limited camera view so cues might be missed.

- Monthly access charges may apply.

Try video meeting interpreting (VMI). Virtual meetings allow you to schedule an interpreter to get on the line with you and facilitate meetings. With increasing international video or Zoom meetings, it is helpful for an interpreter to clarify conversations and understanding. Typically, you schedule the events in advance, so it is easy to schedule an interpreter at the same time. With a little planning, you can hire an interpreter with language and subject matter expertise to make you more productive. Attendees can be at any location around the world if each person has a stable internet connection. Language agencies such as Rapport International know which interpreters have the language, subject matter knowledge, and technical abilities to assist.

Pros:

- Conduct live, virtual business meetings with customers and colleagues who speak different languages.

- Connect more personally than with phone interpreters.

- See facial expressions and visual cues to increase accuracy of communication.

- Schedule easily to meet your time requirements.

- Share your screen so that everyone can see what you are talking about.

- Totally virtual, so participants can be located anywhere around the globe.

Cons:

- Must be scheduled ahead, not an on-demand option.

- Each participant needs access to technology with a camera and internet connection, as well as a platform or app for the video call/conference (like Zoom or GoToMeeting).

- More expensive than telephone or VRI services.

- Confidentiality is only as secure as the platform that you use.

Schedule in-person interpreting. An interpreter participates at the physical location with you to facilitate the conversation. This arrangement is ideal for tours, meals, and certain kinds of meetings and live events. It is the best way to facilitate multilingual communication but the most expensive and difficult to schedule since a trained interpreter fully bilingual in both languages must be able to attend.

Pros:

- Helpful if you need an interpreter for an extended time.

- Easier for reviewing complex content or when things need to be explained in detail.

- No need for any technology like a computer, tablet, or other hardware.

- Better for going over sensitive information, such as medical conditions, confidential information, or negotiations.

- Good choice when you need to use visual cues or if body language is important.

- More personal than electronic connections.

Cons:
- Slightly more expensive since the interpreter must attend.

- Travel expenses and minimum hourly charges might apply.

- Local availability of language or subject-matter expertise can be an issue.

- Appointments must be made in advance.

Hire bilingual employees. Usually, when a company decides to start multilingual marketing, they think they need to hire bilingual employees to handle customer service. That expectation is enough to stop all consideration of multilingual marketing. Hiring the right person for the job is hard enough, let alone looking for a person qualified *and* bilingual in the targeted language. The options mentioned previously, though, give you alternatives that can last quite a while.

Hiring bilingual employees will benefit you eventually…as long as you do it right. As with all employees, any new person needs to fit into the culture, see a career path, be heard, and be recognized. Those expectations mean that you must have a company that celebrates diversity, equity, and inclusion. I could write a whole book on that topic, and in Chapter 18, I will discuss more about this subject so that you will understand how to be successful in developing a culture that can excel in global inbound marketing.

ACTION STEPS:

1. Assess current internal capabilities for providing in-language support.

2. Determine what current service-delivery steps could be standardized, translated, and automated.

3. Decide on the resources needed to deliver human support.

CHAPTER 18

SPOKEN INTERPRETATION OPTIONS

"Everyone smiles in the same language."
—Unknown author

Eventually, you might run out of ways to handle written communications and need a way to speak in more depth with a prospect or client who does not speak your language.

Fortunately, people train to facilitate these conversations. Professional interpreters have intensive training, either by majoring in the profession at college or attending specialized schools. Interpreters must be fully bilingual in two languages and then learn about the profession and the different kinds of interpreting.

When you understand your options and the requirements for becoming an interpreter, you can figure out the best solution for your needs.

SKILLS NEEDED TO PROVIDE PROFESSIONAL QUALITY INTERPRETING SERVICES

High-quality interpreting goes beyond mastery of another language.

A professional interpreter bridges the communication gap between two different cultures and languages. A high-quality, professional interpreter is not only fluent in two languages, but will also possess these important skills and qualities:

- **Listening skills:** Interpreters need to pick up on every word, intent, and meaning. They need to make sense of a message composed in one language while simultaneously constructing the same message in another language.

- **Cultural competence:** Success of an interpreter entails having the ability to pick up nonverbal cues or customs that are specific to a group of people. A strong grasp of cultural norms helps the interpreter convey what the non-native speaker is trying to get across.

- **Emotional resilience:** Interpreters can be exposed to high-profile court cases, highly confidential business meetings, delicate political or emergency medical situations. Despite having to facilitate in these scenarios, interpreters must continually present in a professional manner.

- **Objectivity:** A quality, professional interpreter will never express their opinion about your material and will always remain neutral. They can convey emotions but will not offer their thoughts, opinions, or advice.

- **Ethics:** Interpreters are respectful and maintain confidentiality for all assignment-related information.

- **Knowledge level:** Interpreters work in real time. They cannot rely on a dictionary, Google, or other reference material. Professionally trained interpreters have subject matter expertise and understand the associated vocabulary and lingo.

Those skills are just some of the key requirements for high-quality, professional interpreters. Additionally, good ones have great interpersonal skills and are punctual, polite, respectful, and dedicated to serving.

Professional interpreters bring more than just words to a complex situation. This perspective from a professional interpreter will help you to understand why.

WHY IT IS BEST TO USE A PROFESSIONAL INTERPRETER VERSUS OTHER BILINGUAL STAFF OR FAMILY MEMBERS

As both a professional interpreter and a family member of a non-English speaker, let me provide insight as to why you should always use a professional.

Having been an interpreter for the last 12 years, I have had countless conversations with both service providers and patients/customers, regarding the importance of a professional interpreter. In these conversations, there seems to be a recurring question that comes up from the service provider perspective, "Why should I pay for a professional interpreter when I can get a family member to do it for free?" Allow me to share with you a personal experience.

Being married to a non-native English speaker, I often accompany my spouse to her various appointments, whether medical or whatever is needed at that moment. At these appointments, I catch myself not acting as I would if I were working, but instead acting as a family member (imagine that?!). Instead of working as a bridge to help fill the gap between the provider and the recipient, in this case my wife, I tend to work more as a filter. I unconsciously end up interjecting my own thoughts as to what the issue might be, and I do not necessarily end up interpreting all the information that is said from one party to another. I, in my own mind, determine what is important or relevant and only pass along that information. That is one of the most common issues that arise when using a family member to interpret instead of a professionally trained interpreter.

If you decide to try to use a bilingual staff member, you will not only run into these types of problems, but also ones to do with the issue of confidentiality. Professional interpreters are educated on the HIPAA rules and regulations and are typically covered under their agency's confidentiality agreements.

With a professionally trained interpreter, you can rest assured that they have been trained to respond in a way that withholds their opinion and transmits an impartial message. They are also trained to interpret exactly what is said and not omit "unimportant" information so that the recipient gets complete and accurate information. In short, the use of untrained interpreters, bilingual staff, or family members increases your odds of making mistakes, missing information, misinformation, violating confidentiality, and the risk of worse outcomes. Professional interpreters are more likely to increase patient or client satisfaction, improve adherence and outcomes, as well as reduce adverse events. So, for everybody's benefit, do not use staff, friends, or family members, use professionally trained interpreters.

Author: Chris Allende, a Rapport International interpreter

WHAT KIND OF INTERPRETER DO YOU NEED?

The first question you might be asked when you request an interpreter is whether you need a simultaneous or consecutive interpreter. Picture the United Nation's (UN) interpreters to get an image of a simultaneous interpreter...people who wear headsets and sit in a booth in the back of the room. As the presenter speaks, they repeat the message in another language in real time. A consecutive interpreter repeats the message when the speaker pauses. In business, consecutive interpreting is typical for discussions, meetings, facility tours, and social engagements.

Once you ask for consecutive interpreting, your options include in-person, phone, and video.

HOW TO COMMUNICATE WITH AN INTERPRETER

When you speak through a simultaneous or consecutive interpreter, you will be more effective if you understand what you can do to communicate your message clearly.

Here are some practical tips for working effectively with an interpreter:

- **Hire a professional.** Look for a professionally trained, experienced interpreter with expertise in your area.

- **Meet with the interpreter.** It is always a good idea to meet with the interpreter before the session to discuss briefly what you will be talking about.

- **Look for cultural guidance from your interpreter.** Your interpreter can help you with more than just words. If you have questions about how to communicate with a particular audience or about the culture, just ask.

- **Speak directly to the other person.** Talk to the client directly, not to the interpreter. Instead of saying, "Ask her when her birthday is," speak directly to the non-English speaker using first-person language: "When is your birthday?" A non-English speaker might understand more English than he/she can express. Vocal intonations, facial expressions, and body language still convey a great deal of information regardless of language barrier.

- **Make eye contact.** Look at the other person or at the audience, not the interpreter. And, maintain eye contact. Also, speak clearly and distinctly so that the interpreter can understand you.

- **Sensitive issues.** Be sensitive to cultural and/or religious differences. Consider the situation and the non-English speaker when deciding whether a male or female interpreter would be appropriate for an interpreting session. In some cultures, female interpreters might not feel comfortable interpreting for male clients.

- **Provide materials in advance.** If you have materials that the interpreter can review before the assignment, provide them in advance. Interpreters like to do a good job, so they will review materials to prepare.

- **Communicate and receive feedback.** During breaks, take a few minutes with the interpreter to get and give any feedback. Develop hand signals to speed up or slow down, or for other messages that you want to communicate.

Additional suggestions particular to consecutive interpreting:

- **Pause for interpretation.** Do not forget to pause after three or four sentences to give the interpreter an opportunity to interpret what you have said. The more you speak without giving the interpreter a moment to interpret, the greater the chance is that the interpreter will miss some important details.

- **Time allocation.** Be patient and schedule time appropriately. Interpreting will take longer than speaking directly to an audience without an interpreter. Think about it as if you need to say everything twice and reflect that in the amount of time scheduled for the meeting.

A few final suggestions to avoid mistakes:

- Do not hire family, friends, children under 18 years old, clients, visitors, or untrained volunteers who might have a conflict of interest.

- Remember that local distributors might not fully understand the cultural context of your meaning, so be wary of using them to interpret.

- Communicate any feedback to your agency. If you like an interpreter, you can ask for that person again. If you did not click with an interpreter for any reason, let the agency know so that they can give training to the interpreter or send someone else next time.

When I speak to clients or at events, I like to start the presentation with this question: "How many languages does a person need to speak to be successful in global marketing?" Usually, I get blank stares and then maybe someone will answer, "Two." My punchline is, "You only need to speak one. If you have a good language services agency, you can speak to anyone in the world."

ACTION STEPS:

1. Identify times in the buyer or client journey when an interpreter would help.

2. Define the resources to support your needs.

CHAPTER 19

INTERNAL DIVERSITY, EQUITY, AND INCLUSION IMPROVES YOUR GLOBAL REACH

*"No circumstance in the natural world is more inexplicable than
the diversity of form and color in the human race."*
—Mary Somerville, the "Queen of the Sciences"

E ven if you faithfully follow the suggestions in each chapter and perfectly implement your global marketing, it will suffer if you fail to think about diversity, equity, and inclusion in the culture of your company.

COMMON MISTAKES

Even companies with good intentions make these 10 mistakes:

1. **Expecting all employees to speak English.** Many employers think that if they hire non-English speakers, they can offer English classes and eventually everyone will speak English. Not everyone has the capability to learn another language but they might be highly skilled in performing the job.

REMEMBER: Making a few adjustments in how you communicate can dramatically increase your employee pool.

2. **Assuming that we are all the same.** Thinking that everybody in the company understands and operates within the norms of the White American culture rather than accepting, appreciating, and learning from other cultures.

> REMEMBER: The benefits of diverse thinking bring better solutions.

3. **Communicating in one style**. In the US, we get directly to the point—the goal reigns supreme. In other cultures, people value relationships more, and the goal might take a back seat to preserve the relationship.

> REMEMBER: Value different ways of communicating.

4. **Recognizing the individual**. In the US, we celebrate and reward individual achievement. In more collective societies, the group makes decisions and reaches goals together. Accomplishments might take longer, but the group works together to move forward. Consensus is most important.

> REMEMBER: Be aware of the dynamics of all the cultures involved and marry them together for best outcomes.

5. **Understanding the hierarchy.** In some places, you would never question your boss. What your boss says, you do. In other cultures, employees can speak up if they do not agree with the boss. Being aware of such differences helps you to encourage feedback before making a mistake.

> REMEMBER: Find ways to hear *all* voices!

6. **Expecting the individual to speak for the group.** Assuming an individual can speak for their whole race/culture is a common mistake. Statements like, "Hey, you speak Spanish…" or "Hey, you're Black…" or "What does your culture think about this?" are insulting and ignorant. If you are White, would you be able to answer, "Hey, what do White people think about this?" Respect people as individuals who have their own viewpoint. They cannot speak for their race or culture.

> REMEMBER: Value the uniqueness of individuals and

personal perspectives.

7. **Promoting only one color.** Without managers and mentors who match the diversity in your company, management will be unaware of issues that can arise. If you have many BIPOC (Black, Indigenous, people of color) employees, but your management is all White, you are not truly embracing equity and your company's performance will suffer. Moreover, prospective BIPOC employees who view your website will see pictures of the management team and might not apply due to the message they receive.

   REMEMBER: Promote according to skills, training, and measurable accomplishments, not by friendships or likeness.

8. **Eliminating hiring biases.** Be wary of discriminatory hiring when looking for qualified candidates. Standard interview processes, like building rapport over shared experiences and colleges, might reveal unconscious bias.

   REMEMBER: Seek out differences to enhance your company's performance.

9. **Disregarding cultural differences.** Holidays, prayer practices, food preferences, and family responsibilities can vary dramatically amongst cultures. Equality means equal; equity means fair. By not offering opportunities for people to practice their cultural norms and traditions, you will lose good staff and applicants.

   REMEMBER: Keep equity (fariness) in company policies to allow for cultural differences.

10. **Promoting subjectively.** Not having clear and objective criteria for promotions can lead to subjective promotions. Without clarity, a company can end up with the dominant culture at the top and bitter feelings among those being passed over for no clear reason.

   REMEMBER: Have clear criteria for promotions.

All these mistakes can be solved with intentional, thoughtful, and clear planning. All research and statistics show that diverse companies perform better. Service Corps of Retired Executives (SCORE), the government-supported, small-business advisory organization, summarized the data.

Key points include:

- Companies with above-average diversity earned 45 percent of revenue from innovation, whereas those with below-average diversity earned only 26 percent.

- Businesses with more diverse management teams have 19 percent *higher* revenue due to innovation.

- Diverse companies are 21 to 33 percent more likely to *out* perform; non-diverse companies are 29 percent more likely to *under* perform.

- Diverse organizations make decisions two times faster with half the number of meetings and deliver 60 percent better results because of fact-based decision making.

- Employees want a diverse workforce. Interestingly, 57 percent think their company should be doing more to increase diversity, and 72 percent would consider leaving an organization for a more inclusive one.[48]

The huge advantage of having a diverse workforce while expanding globally is increased sensitivity to inclusion and the value of differences. With the current focus on diversity, equity, and inclusion, you can find plenty of information on the internet to learn and, better yet, listen to voices of those different from you on how to improve in your own organization. Here, I describe experiences of leaders who did just that.

SUCCESS STORIES

IBM stripped personal information such as name, location, and school name from resumes, so recruiters looked only at objective skills and facts, which avoided unconscious bias and opened the door for inclusivity.[49]

Other experiences of companies that created ways to open their culture and be more diverse, equitable, and inclusive (and thus benefited):

- Years ago, a client, Tufts Health Plan, recognized that the demographics of the New England region were changing at a rapid pace. To successfully live its mission of improving the health and wellness of the diverse communities it serves, they established a company-wide Business Diversity program to strengthen and enhance their clinical programs and the member experience for their diverse populations. The program, led by Juan Lopera, reports to senior management and the board of directors on a wide range of workforce, marketplace, and community initiatives to meet the needs of racial and ethnic minorities; women; lesbian, gay, bisexual, transgendered, and queer or questioning (LGBTQ); people with disabilities; and veterans. Over the years, the company gained a reputation as the employer of choice, and the business diversity program has won several awards and accolades for their work on behalf of their members, their community, and their workforce. Juan's role expanded in the last several years to include marketing, business development, and community relations for all products offered by Tufts Health Plan's public plans division across Massachusetts and Rhode Island.

- The marketing team at Pepperidge Farm could not entice the US Latino market to buy their products, so management asked Latino employees, "Why do Latinos not buy our cookies?" Interestingly, several employees suggested that strawberry cookies might increase their appeal with the Latino market. Pepperidge Farm made a strawberry cookie, and guess what? It flew off the shelves, particularly in Latino-dominant areas.

- Myles Meyers founded Superbia Services Inc. to provide fair treatment and equal access to banking, life and health insurances, and financial services to over 16 million Americans identifying as the LGBTQ community. Members of the community are marginalized and excluded by systemic LGBTQ intolerance and discrimination in these industries. Superbia affirms LGBTQ individuals and offers the unique products/services to meet LGBTQ needs and to accelerate economic and social equality of the LGBTQ community. Superbia is quickly growing and well on the way to becoming the iconic financial services brand of the LGBTQ (and allied) community.

- A California-based leadership-training company came to us for the translation of their website. Even though the global leaders they trained spoke English as a second language very well, the company realized that the unique names used to describe their specialty services on their website were not as clear to non-native speakers as much as to native English speakers. By translating the names and the content to capture the meaning and essence of why their trainings developed better leaders, the company won more business. Eventually, they translated their PowerPoint presentations into multiple languages to make sure the leaders really learned.

- As a manufacturer of specialty metal rods used in medical devices, Boston Centerless needs qualified and trained employees who pay attention to precision. Management realized that many of their best employees had limited English skills, so they asked those employees for referrals. Employees recruited their friends and family to work with them. The success of Boston Centerless depended on keeping the employees so they developed an equitable and inclusive workplace. From training, promoting, recognizing, and celebrating, they experienced great success in having a multilingual and multicultural workplace.

> To learn more about how they did this, read more at:
> www.rapporttranslations.com/blog/inclusion-diversity-boston-centerless.

Since Boston Centerless has a successful track record in diversity, equity, and inclusion, I think it is worthwhile to look at their suggestions and outcomes.

After years of experience working across cultures, the managers at Boston Centerless recommend these 10 things:

1. Making sure that supervisors or managers understand the culture enough to know when someone really gets it versus nodding in polite agreement. A head nod in different cultures might not have the same meaning.

2. Having managers and supervisors who can serve as language facilitators and cultural brokers. Miscommunication can happen when someone does not understand the language and culture.

3. Promoting on ability and objective measures to truly make your company culturally welcoming. If all your managers are one race and all your workers are another, expect a chasm.

4. Checking, before hiring, to ensure that new employees have the basic skills to do the job. At Boston Centerless, everyone needs to have math skills to monitor quality.

5. Focusing on "the numbers" to avoid mistakes, miscommunication, and disagreements. When the team focuses on quality metrics, production numbers, financial goals, or other numbers, everyone understands the objective goals. Management can base rewards, recognition, and promotions on measurable accomplishments.

6. Building a performance culture. Without a focus on performance, people tend to get sloppy or be unsure of expectations.

7. Communicating important information in all languages. If you do not have bilingual or multilingual employees, hire experts. In-person interpreters or telephone interpreters are worth the cost in the long run.

8. Encouraging teamwork. Teamwork produces natural peer pressure to work hard to achieve goals. Employees prefer teammates who will not drag them down.

9. Rewarding trustworthiness. Having trustworthy employees and coworkers means the job will get done right.

10. Screening employees and training them well. Just hiring non-English speakers will not be enough. You must have a plan to help them succeed.

Both the effort of creating a diverse workforce and working through the accompanying challenges paid off for Boston Centerless. Their culture is inclusive and celebratory. Individuals and teams are recognized. The company has:

- A very loyal workforce. The company displays many pictures of retired employees who worked for the firm for well over 20 years, and over half the current workforce has been with the company for more than five years. Employees appreciate the chance for long-term, well-paying employment at an organization with an inclusive culture that focuses on quality and continuous improvement.

- Appreciative staff. Statistically, educated immigrants in the US who do not speak English find limited job prospects. Boston Centerless offers engaging work with lots of opportunities for learning and growth. In return, its employees appreciate the opportunity and inclusive culture.

- Limited open positions. In an economy where manufacturers

struggled to find employees, Boston Centerless did not. Employees continually referred qualified friends and family for open positions.

- A model factory. Other manufacturers tour the Boston Centerless facility because it is known to be an effective factory in hiring, training, cleanliness, employee retention, and productivity, all of which makes people proud to work there.

- Competitively high salaries. Boston Centerless' clients pay a premium for their high-quality work, which allows the company to pay a premium on wages.

- Long-term success. The company just celebrated 60 years in business and is going strong.

After we provided translation for them, I had the opportunity to visit Boston Centerless. While walking through the shop floor, I could feel the employee engagement and satisfaction. I saw first-hand the objective measures in place for merit promotions and raises, and quickly understood the recognition programs instituted to acknowledge jobs well done.

FINAL WORDS

"The past cannot be changed. The future is yet in your power."
—*Mary Pickford, American-Canadian film actress, founder*
of the Motion Picture Academy

I want to leave you with a story about a client of ours that continues to experience success with global marketing. Their story exemplifies the opportunities that I talk about throughout the book.

Numberall Stamp & Tool has been designing, manufacturing, and servicing a complete line of quality marking equipment since 1930. Based in Maine, with about 50 employees and about $10 million in revenue, the company sells all over the world (www.numberall.com/).

From the 1950s to the 1980s, the company advertised in print publications such as *Modern Machine Shop, Cutting Tool Engineering*, and others that no longer exist. Sometimes buyers from other countries contacted them for their specialty manufacturing. When buyers did not speak their language, they used pictures and diagrams to communicate.

In the 1980s, an engineer from Columbia joined their team and facilitated communications with Spanish-speaking buyers. After he left, they resumed their fractured communications.

In 2014, through their marketing agency, Pulse Creative, they contacted Rapport International for website translation as they thought we could provide a high quality and professional translation. They knew that by providing answers on their website to commonly asked questions, they could simplify the buying process for Spanish speakers.

After launching the Spanish-language site, they saw an increase in queries for their products and shortened the time to closing sales with Spanish-speaking buyers. In addition, they experienced growth with more repeat business and new clients.

The company's vice president, Daniel Bayerdorffer, says that they saw an increase in visitors to their Spanish language site after it launched. They continue to add Spanish language blogs so that search engines show their company when buyers search their key words or terms. "We see a spike of visitors whenever we post a popular Spanish blog," says Bayerdorffer.

As for providing customer service in Spanish or other languages, he says, "For more complicated orders, we might have to use telephone interpreting, but for right now, we can close sales over email by using Google Translate."

Numberall is considering adding landing pages translated into Arabic, French, German, and other languages to increase business in other parts of the world.

After their experience and successful track record, they are well-positioned to grow internationally.

If they can do it, so can you.

Enjoy the road and please keep in touch by sharing your experiences—the funny, good, dangerous, and learning opportunities. I am always here to support you in your venture.

@wendypease
www.linkedin.com/in/wendypease/
www.facebook.com/wendypease
www.instagram.com/wendy.pease
www.wendypease.com
www.RapportTranslations.com
Clubhouse @WendyPease

For a free consultation: www.rapporttranslations.com/request-a-consultation

To sign up for Language Tidbits: www.rapporttranslations.com/subscribe-to-tidbits

Listen to interviews with experts on The Global Marketing Show podcast: www.TheGlobalMarketingShow.com

RESOURCES

UNITED STATES FEDERAL RESOURCES:

- US Export Initiative: www.trade.gov/export-solutions
- A Resource on Strategic Trade Management and Export Controls: www.state.gov/bureaus-offices/under-secretary-for-arms-control-and-international-security-affairs/bureau-of-international-security-and-nonproliferation/office-of-export-control-cooperation/
- Federal Exporting Trade Assistance: ustr.gov/trade-topics/trade-toolbox/export-assistance
- Office of International Trade: www.sba.gov/about-sba/sba-locations/headquarters-offices
- US Department of Commerce, Bureau of Industry and Security: www.bis.doc.gov
- US Census Bureau, Foreign Trade: www.census.gov/foreign-trade/index.html
- US International Trade Commission: www.usitc.gov
- US Trade Representative: ustr.gov
- US Customs and Border Protection: www.cbp.gov
- Export-Import Bank of the United States: www.exim.gov
- Overseas Private Investment Corporation: www.opic.gov

STATE RESOURCES

- US Export Assistance Agencies by State: 2016.export.gov/usoffices/index.asp
- State Trade and Export Promotion (STEP) Program Fact Sheet: www.sba.gov/content/state-trade-and-export-promotion-fact-sheet

INFORMATION/STATISTICAL RESOURCES

- International Trade Administration, TradeStats Express: tse.export.gov/tse/tsehome.aspx
- USDA Foreign Agricultural Service: www.fas.usda.gov
- United Nations Comtrade Database: comtrade.un.org
- globalEDGE: globaledge.msu.edu
- CIA, The World Factbook: www.cia.gov/library/publications/the-world-factbook/

INDUSTRY KNOWLEDGE

Donald A. DePalma and Paul O'Mara, "Can't Read, Won't Buy – B2C Analyzing Consumer Language Preferences and Behaviors in 29 Countries," CSA Research, www.csa-research.com, June 2020

RECOMMENDED BOOKS:

Traction: Get a Grip on Your Business by Gino Wickman (Dallas, TX: BenBella, 2012). He gives a clearly defined roadmap on how set a direction for your company.

Inbound Marketing: Attract, Engage, and Delight Customers Online by Brian Halligan and Dharmesh Shah (Hoboken, NJ: Wiley, 2014).

Inbound Organization: How to Build and Strengthen Your Company's Future Using Inbound Principles by Dan Tyre and Todd Hockenberry (Hoboken, NJ: Wiley, 2017).

Inbound Content: A Step-by-Step Guide to Doing Content Marketing the Inbound Way by Justin Champion (Hoboken, NJ: Wiley, 2018)

They Ask You Answer: A Revolutionary Approach to Inbound Sales, Content Marketing, and Today's Digital Consumer by Marcus Sheridan (Hoboken, NJ: Wiley, 2017).

Scaling Up: How a Few Companies Make It...and Why the Rest Don't by Verne Harnish (Ashburn, VA: Gazelles, 2014)

GLOSSARY

Crowdsourcing Translation: Done by whoever is available to translate. It is fast and cheap, but offers no guarantee on quality, consistency, confidentiality, ownership, or control of message.

Cultural Adaptation: A globalized translation that is culturally adapted for an audience. For example, the US Department of Public Health hired Rapport International to translate an educational brochure for new mothers. In the English version, we included pictures of mothers of different races; Latina mothers populated the brochure's Brazilian Portuguese and US Spanish versions. The message was the same, but the visuals were adapted for the audience. Chapter 16 is dedicated to cultural adaptation.

Globalization: A more specific term for translation that can be used across different geographic areas that speak the same language. For example, a quality Spanish translation of a technical manual for a manufacturing company could be used in Argentina, Venezuela, and Spain.

Interpreting: Verbal communication across different languages. Consecutive is good for doctor appointments, depositions, small meetings. The interpreter repeats the information in each language. Simultaneous is used in conferences where the information is interpreted in real time. Think of interpreters at the UN, sitting in booths, interpreting in real time with the audience wearing headsets.

Localization: Another specific term for a quality translation that considers cultural references, traditions, local currency, and familiar sports figures/actors for a specific target audience. For example, Adidas soccer ball advertisements around the world use different team colors, sports figures, and display relative currencies. Localization is more expensive and more difficult to manage, yet it creates deep connections with targeted buyers.

Machine Translation: Programmed translation (through AI or an algorithm) that attempts to provide quality yet falls short of human translation.

Good for emails in a foreign language; not good enough yet for marketing translation. Read more about machine translation in Chapter 7 and visit our website to watch the video about Google Translate: www.rapporttranslations.com/videos/google-translate-plugin-issues.

Multilingual Chat: Providing a chat function, which is growing in popularity, to offer client support through a web texting box. Chat can be provided via automated answers, called a chatbot. It is easy to translate and activate once the bot is set up in the first language. Or a company can have a live person monitor the chat feature and respond to questions, known as live chat, which takes training and experience on company knowledge and the ability to respond quickly in the preferred language. Companies that do not have employees to handle live responses in multiple languages use outsourcing to chat services companies, the way businesses use call centers. At Rapport International, we offer both chatbot translation and live multilingual chat. This begets the fun question: "Is it translation or interpretation?" Since chats are written responses, they could be called translation, yet they are also live and direct, which is interpretation.

Telephone Interpreting: Inexpensive and on-demand consecutive interpreting over the phone, usually billed by the amount of time that the interpreter is on the phone. It is best for short calls and meetings.

Transcreation: Text created specifically for instances when there is no content on this subject or the original message will not translate or adapt. For example, we offer an English-language pricing package for foreign companies looking to expand into the US that includes a brochure, website, fact sheet, and investor deck. The message and look of the materials undergo "transcreation" from the original language and format so that companies can speak directly to US investors and clients. In that case, localization is not enough; the materials are transformed to deeply connect with the US market.

Transcription: Converts spoken language into a written document. And, yes, it is in the same language. To add a voice-over or subtitles to a video, we need the recording ready for transcription or a transcription of an audio file to provide to the translator. It takes longer to translate from an audio file, so transcribing the audio file first saves time.

Translation: Conversion of written text *and* meaning by a bilingual person from one language into another language. With the right translator, you can convey your message culturally and in the correct context (more on this in Chapter 7). Excellent for global inbound.

Transliteration: Conversion of words or letters from one script or alphabet to another with little to no regard for sound, meaning, or intent. Sometimes called "word to word" translation. Not helpful in global inbound marketing.

Simultaneous Virtual Event Interpreting: Needs an interpreting platform that works in conjunction with the event platform. Attendees can choose their language and hear in real time the speaker's message, no matter which language is spoken.

Video Meeting Interpreting: A consecutive interpreter that logs in to your video meeting to assist with the discussion. All participants can be in any location. An interpreter can be added on to any platform that the organization chooses.

Video Remote Interpreting (VRI): Consecutive interpreting through a video monitor when both parties are in one room. VRI is becoming more accessible and on demand. The platform must be secure and confidential.

ACKNOWLEDGMENTS

Olivia Gieg – You published "Medicine of the Mind" when you were a teenager. You were a huge motivation for me to write and publish a book. Thank you for being you.

Lisa Rea – Thank you for your marketing brilliance, consistent friendship, and honest feedback. And thank you for the many words you contributed to the book. You are a joy to work with and know.

Linda Spooner – You are my rock. My gratitude for all you do, every day, year over year encourages me to do and be better. Thank you for inspiring and teaching me.

The Team – Vicki, Aimi, Ann Marie, Jennifer, Linda C. and Nathan – you guys ROCK! Thank you for caring for our clients so carefully. I LOVE all the compliments I get about YOU!

Mom – Thanks for letting me tell the story about the Chinese translation! And I appreciate your feedback on version one. Love you!

Sharon Heimbaugh – Nothing in my life happens without you knowing about it. Thank you for being you and making me a better person. Love you!

Sarah Ginand – Where would I be without your insightful, calming, practical and consistent business advice! You are a true bright spot in my life. (By the way, if anyone reading this needs a great marketing strategist, you can find Sarah at www.smcboston.com/about)

Brian Morris – What a pleasure to work with you on the audio recording. (If anyone needs a consummate professional to record an audio book, interview, or podcast, I highly recommend him - https://www.linkedin.com/in/brian-morris-b321197/.)

Nancy Marks – Your advice on the early copy was helpful! Thanks for helping me swim through to completion.

Dan Tyre and David Weinhaus – The dynamic duo who builds the LIONS up from cubs to a roaring pride. The knowledge, teamwork, and support you bring is rewarding and motivating in so many ways!

Alicia Marie – I've moved from "desire" to "peace" since working with you. Thank you for your steady coaching, support, and friendship.

My boys – Robert and David. You are amazing young men who inspire me continually in all areas of my life. You've taught me so much and made my life incredibly wonderful. You are the best, you are my heart, and I love you to the moon and beyond. Stay as fun, curious, kind, and adventurous as you are!

ENDNOTES

1 Nataly Kelly, "Speak to Global Customers in Their Own Language," Harvard Business Review, July 23, 2014, https://hbr.org/2012/08/speak-to-global-customers-in-t.

2 "US EXPORTING FACTS—Big or Small, You Can Export," California Inland Empire District Export Council, http://www.ciedec.org/resources/exporting-facts/.

3 "Infographic: Small Business, Big Trade," SCORE, March 21, 2019, https://www.score.org/resource/infographic-small-business-big-trade.

4 "US Export Fact Sheet," International Trade Administration, April 5, 2016, https://legacy.trade.gov/press/press-releases/2016/export-factsheet-040516.pdf.

5 HubSpot, "2020 Marketing Statistics, Trends & Data - The Ultimate List of Digital Marketing Stats,"https://www.hubspot.com/marketing-statistics.

6 Chris Lake, "The Rise of 'Micro-Moments' and How to Optimise for 'near Me' Search Queries," Search Engine Watch, November 28, 2019, https://www.searchenginewatch.com/2016/03/29/the-rise-of-micro-moments-and-how-to-optimise-for-near-me-search-queries/.

7 Janet Grynberg, "Consumer Insights Roundup: 87% of Shoppers Begin Product Searches Online, 52% of U.S. Teens Cut Back on Mobile Phone Use," Portada, August 24, 2018, https://www.portada-online.com/new-research-stats/consumer-insights-roundup-87-of-shoppers-begin-product-searches-online-52-of-u-s-teens-cut-back-on-mobile-phone-use/.

8 "SBA Helps Nations Oldest Ice Cream Company Tap Exploding International Markets," US Small Business Administration, n.d., https://www.sba.gov/offices/district/pa/king-of-prussia/success-stories/sba-helps-nations-oldest-ice-cream-company-tap-exploding-international-markets.

9 "Faces of Trade: Rekluse Motor Sports," U.S. Chamber of Commerce, January 21, 2015, https://www.uschamber.com/faces-trade-rekluse-motor-sports.

10 Chris Isadore, "These Are the Top US Exports," CNNMoney (CNN, March 7, 2018), https://money.cnn.com/2018/03/07/news/economy/top-us-exports/index.html.

11 Ibid.

12 Jasmine Enberg, "Global Digital Ad Spending 2019," Insider Intelligence (Insider Intelligence, March 28, 2019), https://www.emarketer.com/content/global-digital-ad-spending-2019.

13 Anthony Cilluffo and Neil G. Ruiz, "World Population Growth Is Expected to Nearly Stop by 2100," May 30, 2020, https://www.pewresearch.org/fact-tank/2019/06/17/worlds-population-is-projected-to-nearly-stop-growing-by-the-end-of-the-century/.

14 Cilluffo, "World Population Growth Is Expected to Nearly Stop by 2100."

15 Prableen Bajpai, "The Five Fastest Growing Economies In The World," Nasdaq, October 16, 2020, https://www.nasdaq.com/articles/the-five-fastest-growing-economies-in-the-world-2020-10-16.

16 https://ourworldindata.org/what-are-ppps

17 "Cost of Living Comparison Between India and the United States," Numbeo, https://www.numbeo.com/cost-of-living/compare_countries_result.jsp?country1=India.

18 "Top 10 Economies 2100 Projections (GDP PPP)," YouTube (Dr. Top Ten, June 2, 2019), https://www.youtube.com/watch?v=E_JhaSTIRUIr.

19 Andrew Sebastian, "Which 10 Countries Have the Highest Incomes?," Investopedia, August 29, 2020, https://www.investopedia.com/articles/markets-economy/090616/5-countries-most-money-capita.asp.

20 "Household Disposable Income," OECD, https://data.oecd.org/chart/5NUz.

21 "Strategic Reasons to Export," International Trade Administration | Trade.gov, https://www.trade.gov/strategic-reasons-export.

22 William Booth, "One Nation, Indivisible: Is It History?," The Washington Post (WP Company, February 22, 1998), https://www.washingtonpost.com/wp-srv/national/longterm/meltingpot/melt0222.htm.

23 "The Numbers of Spanish Speakers in the World Exceeds 500 Million," Spanish Language Domains, July 26, 2014, https://spanishlanguagedomains.com/the-numbers-of-spanish-speakers-in-the-world-exceeds-500-million/.

24 "English to Spanish Translations: Translate English to Spanish," Hispanic Market Solutions: Language, Search, Content, Social, January 4, 2021, https://www.hispanicmarketadvisors.com/english-to-spanish-translation.

25 https://www.pewresearch.org/fact-tank/2015/03/24/a-majority-of-english-speaking-hispanics-in-the-u-s-are-bilingual/

26 "Gains in Translation: What Your Language Choices Say to US Hispanics," Facebook IQ, October 4, 2016, https://www.facebook.com/business/news/insights/gains-in-translation-what-your-language-choices-say-to-us-hispanics.

27 Lisa Gevelber, "Your Next Big Opportunity: The U.S. Hispanic Market," Think with Google (Google, July 2014), https://www.thinkwithgoogle.com/future-of-marketing/digital-transformation/us-hispanic-market-digital/.

28 Laurel Wentz, "Ad Age's 2017 Hispanic Fact Pack Is Out Now," Ad Age, August 28, 2017, https://adage.com/article/cmo-strategy/ad-age-s-2017-hispanic-fact-pack/310224/.

29 "Help Small Businesses to Export," U.S. Chamber of Commerce, July 24, 2019, https://www.uschamber.com/issue-brief/help-small-businesses-export.

30 Jamie Ducharme, "Why Do They Speak French at the Olympics Closing Ceremony," Time (Time, February 26, 2018), https://time.com/5174937/french-olympics-closing-ceremonies/.

31 Ethnologue, Languages of the World, https://www.ethnologue.com/about.

32 Nataly Kelly, "Speak to Global Customers in Their Own Language," Harvard Business Review, July 23, 2014, https://hbr.org/2012/08/speak-to-global-customers-in-t.

33 "User language preferences online," European Commision, May 2011, https://ec.europa.eu/commfrontoffice/publicopinion/flash/fl_313_en.pdf

34 Deyan Georgiev, "111+ Revealing Google Statistics and Facts To Know In 2020," Review42, November 21, 2020, https://review42.com/google-statistics-and-facts/.

35 J. Clement, "Global Online Search Query Search Platform Share 2020," Statista, August 31, 2020, https://www.statista.com/statistics/413229/search-query-size-search-engine-share/.

36 Monika Markovinovic, "Yes, This Shopping App Is Actually Selling 'Fat Lady' Clothes," HuffPost Canada, March 23, 2016, https://www.huffingtonpost.ca/2016/03/22/wish-fat-lady_n_9523066.html.

37 "What Is Nike's Mission?," Nike, https://www.nike.com/help/a/nikeinc-mission.

38 Tex Texin, "Marketing Translation Mistakes," Internationalization (I18n), Localization (L10n), Standards, and Amusements, http://www.i18nguy.com/translations.html.

39 Ibid.

40 "11 Brand Names That Sound Really Wrong in Foreign Language," Marketing. Shmarketing, April 12, 2015, https://marketingshmarketing.tumblr.com/post/116199876011/11-brand-names-that-sound-really-wrong-in-foreign.

41 Gilles Castonguay, "Fiat Apologizes to China for TV Ad for New Car," Reuters, June 20, 2008, https://www.reuters.com/article/industry-fiat-china-dc/fiat-apologizes-to-china-for-tv-ad-for-new-car-idINL2030648920080620.

42 "Idioms," The Idioms, https://www.theidioms.com/.

43 Heath Evans, "'Content Is King' - Essay by Bill Gates 1996," Medium, October 28, 2017, https://medium.com/@HeathEvans/content-is-king-essay-by-bill-gates-1996-df74552f80d9.

44 Nicole Flynn, "Top 19 Video Marketing Statistics for 2019," cielo24, January 23, 2019, https://cielo24.com/2019/01/video-marketing-statistics-2019/.

45 Joseph Hernandez, "Hygge Is so 2016. Meet Kalsarikannit, the Word for Drinking at Home without Pants On," Chicago Tribune, July 2, 2019, https://www. chicagotribune.com/dining/drink/ct-hygge-is-so-2016-seven-wines-to-try-story.html.

46 Josh Biggs, "10 International Marketing Campaigns That Failed to Translate," Meldium, August 26, 2020, https://www.meldium.com/10-international-marketing-campaigns-that-failed-to-translate/.

47 Rocio Lorenzo et al., "How Diverse Leadership Teams Boost Innovation," Boston Consulting Group, November 18, 2020, https://www.bcg.com/en-us/ publications/2018/how-diverse-leadership-teams-boost-innovation.

48 "Infographic: How Diversity Drives Business Success," SCORE, November 16, 2020, https://www.score.org/resource/infographic-how-diversity-drives-business-success.

49 "How to Fix Your Tech Interview to Increase Diversity," Diversify Techs, June 16, 2019, https://www.diversifytech.co/blog/how-to-fix-tech-interview-to-increase-diversity.